MICHAEL
CARRIE PETTUS-DAVIS
JEFFREY J. SHOOK

Conducting Research in Juvenile and Criminal Justice Settings

OXFORD
UNIVERSITY PRESS

Oxford University Press, Inc., publishes works that further
Oxford University's objective of excellence
in research, scholarship, and education.

Oxford   New York
Auckland   Cape Town   Dar es Salaam   Hong Kong   Karachi
Kuala Lumpur   Madrid   Melbourne   Mexico City   Nairobi
New Delhi   Shanghai   Taipei   Toronto

With offices in
Argentina   Austria   Brazil   Chile   Czech Republic   France   Greece
Guatemala   Hungary   Italy   Japan   Poland   Portugal   Singapore
South Korea   Switzerland   Thailand   Turkey   Ukraine   Vietnam

Published by Oxford University Press, Inc.
198 Madison Avenue, New York, New York 10016
www.oup.com

Oxford is a registered trademark of Oxford University Press

Library of Congress Cataloging-in-Publication Data

Vaughn, Michael G.
Conducting research in juvenile and criminal justice settings / Michael G. Vaughn,
Carrie Pettus-Davis, Jeffrey J. Shook.
p. cm. — (Pocket guides to social work research methods)
Includes bibliographical references and index.
ISBN 978-0-19-978285-7 (pbk. : alk. paper)   1. Juvenile justice, Administration
of—Research—United States. 2. Juvenile delinquency—Research—United States.
3. Criminal justice, Administration of—Research—United States. 4. Social service—
Research. I. Pettus-Davis, Carrie. II. Shook, Jeffrey J. III. Title.

HV9104.V385 2012
364.36072—dc23   2011040106

1 3 5 7 9 8 6 4 2

Printed in the United States of America
on acid-free paper

Contents

Preface

Despite the impact that the criminal justice system has on client populations served by social workers and related professionals, there are few practical sources available to guide research in these settings. Our goal in writing this book was to fill that gap. As such, technical jargon and gratuitous citing of references, common in journal articles, were kept to a minimum. This book is intended not only for researchers but also for graduate students and agency administrators. It provides state-of-the-art techniques and can be used as a reference guide, in criminal justice and juvenile justice courses, that will facilitate the advancement of knowledge in social work and beyond.

There has been a renewal of interest by researchers in social work in conducting research in criminal and juvenile justice settings. In large part, this interest has been fueled by the tremendous increase in incarceration over the past several decades. For example, the number of individuals incarcerated in state and federal prisons increased from approximately 320,000 in 1980 to more than 1.5 million in 2008 (Glaze, 2010). The jail population grew from approximately 184,000 to 785,000 over the same period and estimates suggest that more than 9 million individuals enter jail each year. In addition, the number of individuals on probation and parole has increased dramatically. Based on a one-day count, more than 7 million adults were under the control of the justice system in 2008. Similar trends have been observed in the juvenile justice system as more youth are formally processed in the juvenile court, detained prior to or after court processing, adjudicated as delinquents, waived to the criminal court, placed on probation, and committed to residential facilities.

The growth of the justice systems poses a number of significant problems. First, expenditures have increased, driven by incarceration and the use of residential placements, placing a strain on state and local budgets and necessitating the development of alternatives to incarceration. Second, the number of individuals reentering society from prisons and jails has increased tremendously. For example, it is estimated that more than 740,000 individuals reenter society each year from state or federal prisons alone (Sabol, West, & Cooper, 2009). According to the Bureau of Justice Statistics and a number of studies, reincarceration rates among these offenders are often over 50%, and approximately two-thirds are rearrested (Langan & Levin, 2002). Importantly, recidivism rates are highest for young offenders (Krisberg & Howell, 1998; Mears & Travis, 2004).

Third, many young people spend a significant amount of their adolescence and young adulthood in correctional facilities (Sickmund, 2004). Contact with the juvenile justice system and incarceration over long swaths of the life-course can influence developmental trajectories (Farrington & Welsh, 2007). This is particularly true for young people who have specific developmental needs that are often not met in the justice systems. Fourth, many offenders face a greater multitude of problems at the personal, family, and community levels (Dembo & Schmeidler, 2003; Petersilia, 2003). These problems often include educational deficiencies and emotional issues such as a history of sexual abuse, physical abuse, and neglect (Cuomo et al., 2008; Dembo, Schmeidler, Nini-gough, & Manning, 1998). They also include high levels of mental health and substance abuse problems (James & Glaze, 2006; Mumula & Karberg, 2006). Furthermore, many offenders come from communities marked by high levels of neighborhood disorder (Jang & Johnson, 2001), concentrated disadvantage (McNulty & Bellair, 2003), and low levels of community collective efficacy[1] (Sampson, Raudenbush, & Earls, 1997).

The enormity and complexity of the problems created by the rise in incarceration are very important to social work. Research in these settings and on these issues is difficult because it requires that researchers not only develop rigorous designs and incorporate a variety of methods, but also navigate a very complex system. Our hope is that this book will fill a major need by providing a cutting-edge yet practical resource for research in these settings. Guidance and examples will span the gamut from conceptualization and design to implementation and analytic strategies. Furthermore, techniques will be provided that have proven to be successful in surmounting the all too critical yet often overlooked barriers to conducting research in these settings, such as gaining Internal Review Board approval. In addition, step-by-step procedures will elucidate the use of extant and administrative data. Practical examples and sample forms and measures will facilitate faster and more effective research implementation. As such, this book will provide a comprehensive resource for social workers and persons in related fields.

As noted previously, there has been a renewed interest among social work researchers in criminal and juvenile justice issues. Many social workers, however, still view these issues as disconnected from other areas of social work research and practice (e.g., mental health, child welfare) or within the purview of other disciplines or professions (e.g., law, criminology). Yet, the trends and problems discussed previously are central concerns to the field. Historically, social work played a significant role in the justice systems profession as being a major contributor to the development and implementation of the juvenile justice system. The overlap of the justice systems with other social service systems is of significant concern to the field as many individuals in these systems drift into justice systems and the consequences of justice system involvement often hinder efforts in these areas. The tremendous increase in spending on the justice systems, in conjunction with decreases in spending on social welfare and education, places strains on state budgets and negatively affects the development of human capital. The substantial overrepresentation of individuals of color and the poor among justice system populations raises serious social justice concerns. The lack of a social work voice in criminal justice matters has, arguably, led to a more law enforcement-oriented approach to criminal justice responses. Consequently, there is a need for an increase in social work research in justice system settings and for the development of a rigorous and vibrant knowledge base within the field regarding these issues.

At the same time, the trends and problems highlighted previously, as well as others, offer real opportunities for social work researchers. For example, the Second Chance Act signed into law by President George W. Bush continues to provide funding for state and local governments to provide reentry services to incarcerated individuals returning to communities. Innovations in responses to crime, such as mental health courts, drug courts, and restorative justice approaches, are increasingly receiving financial support and attention from policy-makers. Thus, there is a need for and interest in the development and testing of interventions designed to decrease recidivism and increase human capital development among individuals leaving correctional settings. Furthermore, these trends provide rich opportunities to build a research-based body of knowledge that can effectively inform practice and influence policy as states are beginning to rethink the policies and practices that have led to the mass incarceration of the past several decades. Given the reality that these issues directly overlap many traditional areas of social work, the increased focus on reentry and community-based alternatives offers a great opportunity for social work researchers to be at the forefront of these efforts.[2]

For social work researchers and other researchers to engage in research in the justice systems, it is imperative that they understand the challenges in place and develop strategies for overcoming these challenges. Conducting research in the justice systems can be difficult due to a variety of factors. At the same time, it can be very fulfilling and meaningful work. The goal of this book is to provide practical techniques and strategies to help researchers learn how to overcome the challenges inherent in conducting research in the justice systems. In keeping with this goal, we kept the technical jargon to a minimum. We hope the book serves as a starting point to developing the tools and skills needed to navigate these systems and inform policy and practice.

Acknowledgments

There are a number of people we would like to thank for seeing this book to its completion. First, we would like to thank the series editor Tony Tripodi and the team at Oxford University Press. They were a pleasure to work with from beginning to end. We would also like to thank our research assistants Ralph Groom, Kristen Peters and Michelle Vance for their hard work on several tedious tasks. Finally, we would like to acknowledge Lenise, Matt, and Sara for their ongoing support.

Conducting Research in Juvenile and Criminal Justice Settings

1

Field Research in Juvenile Justice Settings

INTRODUCTION

Many opportunities exist for scholars to conduct research in juvenile justice settings including pathway studies of arrest and system entry, law enforcement-juvenile relations, individual change in incarcerated settings (state and local), system changes and courts, and aftercare or reentry back to the community. Large numbers of young people enter juvenile courts each year and there are considerable debates regarding the role of the system and how it affects the lives of these young people. For example, there is currently an increased emphasis on community-based programs for youth involved in the juvenile justice system, meaning that there is considerable opportunity to conduct research assessing the effectiveness of these programs including those that serve as alternatives to formal court processing or incarceration (e.g., Howell, 2009). At the same time, there remains a need for research on the characteristics and needs of young people in the juvenile justice system, research on the effectiveness of residential facilities, and research on restorative justice practices. There also remains a need for research on decision making and case processing in juvenile justice settings, especially given the overrepresentation of youth of color in these systems. Although not without many difficulties, research in these settings can also yield important findings that inform theory, policies, and practices.

Despite the need for these, and other, types of studies in juvenile justice settings, there are many challenges to conducting research in the juvenile justice system. This chapter explores these challenges and suggests a number of insights and solutions to problems that often arise in juvenile justice settings including how to gain and maintain Institutional Review Board (IRB) approval, how to manage a project across multiple agencies, courts, and institutions, and how to maintain relationships with key stakeholders. Furthermore, we discuss issues related to planning a research project in juvenile justice settings, including research designs, assessment and measurement, recruitment, and retention. Although many of the areas mentioned in this chapter have not typically involved social work researchers, there is a considerable amount of interesting and important research waiting to be explored. The overall goal of the chapter is to provide sufficient practical information to provide social work researchers with a roadmap for beginning or continuing a research agenda in juvenile justice settings.

MAJOR DOMAINS OF THE JUVENILE JUSTICE SYSTEM

The juvenile justice system consists of a variety of "loosely coupled" agencies, institutions, and actors who all play a particular role in deciding how a case will be handled and what sanctions, services, and programs a youth will receive, if any. Thus, there are many settings in the juvenile justice system in which one can do field research. Researchers interested in the juvenile justice system need to realize that there is considerable variation both across and within states with regard to the structure of the system and the range of sanctions, policies that govern the jurisdiction and operation of the system, programs, and services. The flow chart in Figure 1.1 presents a generalized overview of the juvenile justice process, but it is important for researchers interested in conducting research in

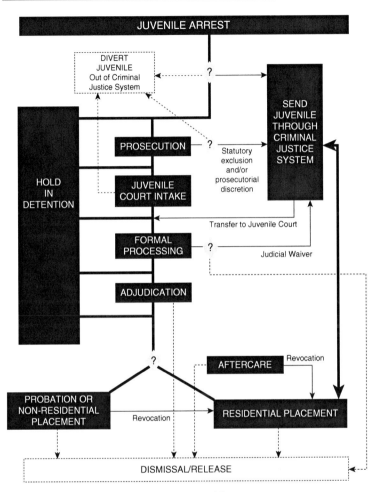

Figure 1.1. Juvenile Justice System Structure and Process.

the juvenile justice system to gain a working understanding of the system in which they plan to do research.

As the flow chart indicates, the beginning of the process is typically the arrest of the juvenile, although young people can also be referred to the court by other actors. Young people can be referred to the juvenile court for offenses or for status offenses (e.g., truancy, incorrigibility), although states differ with regard to how status offenses are handled. Once an arrest is made and a young person is referred to the court, a decision needs to be made about whether to divert the case or file a formal petition in the juvenile court. A variety of actors can be involved in this decision including law enforcement (e.g., police and prosecutors), intake officers, victims, and the youth and his or her parents. There are often specific criteria such as the number of prior contacts with the juvenile justice system and offense that are considered in the decision on whether to divert the case.

If the decision is made to file a petition, a juvenile may be held in a secure detention facility—assuming a hearing by a judge deems the detention to be in the best interest of the community. The majority of petitions are filed in the juvenile court, but each state has mechanisms to transfer a juvenile to the criminal court. In some states, youth are automatically excluded from the jurisdiction of the juvenile court based on specific characteristics (e.g., age, offense). Other states allow the prosecutor to determine whether to file in the juvenile or criminal court. Most states employ judicial waiver mechanisms, often in conjunction with one of the two mechanisms discussed previously, in which the prosecutor files a motion for transfer and a judge makes a determination based on specific criteria following a hearing. If the petition is filed in the juvenile court, due process protections attach (except for the right to trial by jury) and the state must prove beyond a reasonable doubt that the youth committed the offense. Although many cases are adjudicated delinquent, often through a plea agreement, many others are dismissed for lack of evidence or are handled informally where a youth agrees to specific sanctions in lieu of a formal adjudication.

If a juvenile is adjudicated delinquent, a disposition hearing is held and the judge decides whether to order probation, residential treatment (public or private), or another disposition plan such as participation in community-based programs. Many juvenile dispositions are multifaceted: a probation order may include such additional requirements as drug counseling, weekend confinement, and community/victim restitution. If a juvenile is committed to a residential facility, he or she may also be required to participate in aftercare upon release, during which time the juvenile is under the supervision of the court or the juvenile corrections department. In general, most field research data collection occurs in detention settings or residential placement facilities. Other areas involving system processing are more conducive to the use of administrative data (see Chapter 3).

ACCESS: DEVELOPING PARTNERSHIPS

One of the most obvious and important components of developing a research project in the juvenile justice system is gaining access. Whether one is doing primary data collection or using administrative data, without access there is no research project. As will be discussed throughout this book, the key to opening the door and gaining the ability to conduct research in juvenile justice settings is developing partnerships. Contrary to what some researchers believe, juvenile justice administrators and staff are not necessarily anxious to have research investigators interrupting their daily schedules. Research projects require time and resources on behalf of the juvenile justice entity. They also might reveal negative results that reflect poorly on the system. At the same time, however, many juvenile justice administrators and staff are well aware of the value of research and are aware that partnering with a university can lend credibility to their organization. Furthermore, juveniles are typically happy to have a break from their usual routines and interact with persons outside of their setting.

It is essential, then, that researchers interested in working in juvenile justice settings consider the need to build partnerships and plan accordingly. In our experience, there are several points worth keeping in mind— so much so that we consider them guidelines.

- Offer win–win scenarios. Think of the research project as a long-term partnership that can be of value to all, including the juveniles!
- Be aware that you are an intruder and are a guest so to speak (i.e., cooking in someone else's kitchen). As such, be considerate of the

tasks and security issues with which these settings must contend. Safety issues and maintaining order are basic goals in these settings.

- Try not to come off as "the expert." Administrators and staff are not necessarily impressed with university researchers. Keep in mind that many administrators and staff do not necessarily read peer-reviewed journals and typically place more value in having practical experiences with juveniles.
- Inquire about what information is useful to the organization. Go over proposed measures with appropriate administrators and staff and make room for organizational suggestions. Ask leaders in these organizations what they would like to know and what data might be useful to them.
- Disseminate the knowledge in a practical way with administrators and staff. They are a part of the research project and can provide valuable insights on the findings.

These guidelines are consistent with the philosophical and operational tenets of community-based participatory research (CBPR). CBPR is an approach that moves away from outside expertise (i.e., university researchers) entering a given community (e.g., juvenile residential placement or detention center) and laying out a research agenda and instead toward engaging and cultivating relationships and input into the research process (Israel, Schultz, Parker, & Becker, 1998; Minkler, 2005). The community-based as opposed to community-placed research is taken seriously. This approach is thought to be more equitable and ethical than outside-expert research (Minkler, 2005). Although this may be true, the practical importance for researchers is that CBPR enhances "buy-in" from a constituency (e.g., detention center or treatment facility). Because the setting, participants, and researchers, are collaborating together toward a common goal the overall execution and potential for success of the research project are increased. One of the most important engagement techniques aligned with this approach is to ask (and listen!) juvenile justice administrators and staff what they think is important to know. Another technique is to use "we" instead of us or I (as in the researchers) when discussing the research project. At the end of the research project it is important to share study findings with research setting personnel and not merely send them a report or copies of articles that were written. It is also useful to collaborate in determining what next steps for further inquiry are needed. Although consistent with the CBPR, we consider that many of these guidelines and techniques proffered are akin to good manners and represent basic fundamentals of relationship building.

COMMON RESEARCH DESIGNS

A number of research designs are available depending on the aims of the project. The most common is the cross-sectional survey. This design is efficient and inexpensive and can be used for exploratory, descriptive, and correlational aims. Extending the power of a cross-sectional survey researchers can use longitudinal or case-control designs, which enhances the ability to infer causation. However, these designs are more complicated and costly. The ability to track and assess youth over time is critical to unraveling what factors are most influential in affecting specific outcomes. Thus, these types of designs are useful for informing intervention designs. With respect to intervention designs, there are generally three major forms with many variations involved. In general, the simplest intervention test is the single-subject design. It is commonly believed that single-subject designs are not rigorous. This is not necessarily true as the use of comparison controls and meticulous measurement is common in fields such as applied behavior analysis that seek to change the behavior of children with developmental disabilities (Vollmer, Sloman, & Samaha, 2009).

A second design is the pre-post design. The pre-post design is a multiple person intervention test that has the flaw of not having a comparison group. Building on pre-post designs by adding a comparison control group that is meaningful to an intervention test is the hallmark of quasiexperimental designs. Experimental designs add randomization. Most importantly, the execution of the design is what is critical. A poorly executed experiment even with randomization is not as useful as a well-executed quasiexperimental design. An additional consideration is the real world potential or practical significance of an intervention. For example, if a simple and low-cost intervention can yield small positive effects then this can be more important than an extensive and costly intervention that yields larger positive effects. This is because the less expensive and more efficient intervention can potentially be implemented on a much larger scale. Interventions that appeal to a broad constituency (e.g., political orientation) are also more likely to be provided with greater resources and thereby affect a larger number of youth.

ASSESSMENT ISSUES

Often the key starting point for successful programming and policy work in juvenile justice systems involves sound assessment of each youth. Settings vary in terms of the extent and quality of assessment procedures. Many organizations use assessment procedures to meet federal, state, or local mental health and health standards and/or to conduct a risk or needs assessment. The assessment issues practitioners face are often quite similar to what field researchers also must surmount. Quite simply, without reliable and valid assessment in field research the overall study integrity is compromised. So, field researchers need to be aware of the data-gathering assessment procedures in place and select study measures that compliment these assessments, are psychometrically sound, are directly pertinent to the study aims, and are efficient with respect to time. Other considerations also include age and cultural appropriateness.

Getting to know the assessment procedures and what measures are employed at juvenile justice research sites is critically important in deciding which measures to employ. This is important for several reasons. First, the site assessment battery can be used to "break-up" any shared method variance that researchers often encounter with one primary data source. Shared method variance occurs when, for example, study participants are given a self-report survey in which several measures and variables within the survey are used as independent and dependent variables. Other sources (e.g., parental report) can be used to corroborate similar or associated constructs. However, using multiple sources of assessment data on each youth adds additional layers of complexity such as the need to correctly identify each data source with each youth as well as additional data entry and management. It also requires greater cooperation and trust and thus emphasizes the importance of relationship building discussed earlier.

Based on the study aims and the conceptual framework, constructs can be mapped or approximated with various assessments. These assessments can include self-report surveys, performance-based measures such as neuropsychological testing, open-ended qualitative information, and even biospecimens [e.g., salivary cortisol levels, buccal cells for genotyping, functional magnetic resonance imaging (fMRI) results].

Because there is a wide array of assessments available their utilization should be driven not only by the aims and hypotheses of the research study but also by budgetary and time constraints. This does not mean that additional measures cannot be added for exploratory reasons. However, researchers should have a rationale for each measure included in the assessment battery. If researchers cannot use a measure to answer a research question or be employed in an article or technical report then that measure should not be included. Additionally, if the measure or question is time-consuming, inappropriate, or may cause discomfort then serious scrutiny should be applied. Often many of these important decisions can be determined on the basis of pilot testing of the assessment battery. If pilot testing is not feasible with juvenile offenders then it is still very helpful to pilot test with students and discuss questions that worked or seemed awkward. The delivery and structure of the assessment administration can be rehearsed and simulated several times prior to the actual project data collection. Spending additional time in preparation will reduce the potential for systematic error and result in a smoother process.

Researchers have identified a number of salient issues with regard to assessment in juvenile justice settings. One of the largest of these issues is the importance of screening. Screening assessments are short measures that help to identify youth in need of greater help in some area of need such as mental health. In this way, screening assessments in a system act as a filter to "catch" youth with specific problems. The assumption behind screening is that this process results in enhanced efficiency and tailored treatments, which in turn yield more effective intervention with a given youth (see Grisso, Vincent, & Seagrave, 2005). Screening measures, as well as fuller assessments, can screen for one problem or disorder such as Attention Deficit Hyperactivity (e.g., Connors, 1997), whereas a multidimensional measure such as the Massachusetts Youth Screening Inventory screens for multiple problems (Grisso & Barnum, 2000; Grisso, Barnum, Fletcher, Cauffman, & Peuschold, 2001). Screening measures make useful research measures because they are brief and efficient and can be used to represent constructs in post-data collection statistical analyses. The timing of the screening is important, however, as it is probably ideal to administer screening measures when youth enter a facility. These measures can also be used upon leaving a facility not only to examine the psychometric properties and performance of a measure (e.g., test-retest reliability) but also to track changes from baseline and infer program impact.

ACQUIRING AND COMPILING MEASURES

Measures can be obtained in several different ways. One way is to employ measures that have been used in other research studies. These studies, typically published in peer-reviewed articles, provide a good starting point for deciding which measures to employ (see the annotated bibliography in Chapter 2). Some measures are commercially available and can be expensive to use on a large scale. One resource for acquiring measures of this kind is available from companies such as Multi-Health Systems (www.mhs.com). Many of these commercially available measures have fairly strong psychometric properties and have demonstrated usefulness. Measures can also be requested from the measure developer with the understanding that they will be used strictly for research purposes. Developers of measures are often eager for other researchers to use their instruments. Researchers can also write their own questions, modify extant measures, and design open-ended response formats. In our own work we have found it useful to develop and build a "wish list" of potential measures that are tied directly to the study goals and then begin the process of removing measures based on criteria such as time and budget constraints, setting input, knowledge of the sample participants, and other unique contextual features. Finally, based on prior studies, it is important to research, evaluate, and report the major domains of reliability (internal consistency reliability, test–retest reliability, and interrater reliability or interrater agreement with chance correction) and validity (concurrent, divergent, predictive, and construct) for measures that form your assessment battery.

THINKING ABOUT THE FUTURE

It is worth mentioning that researchers should have an eye to the future when developing study protocols and implementing a research plan. These considerations include the expansion of a study and what data, design, personnel issues, and human subjects requirements (discussed later in this chapter) will be needed. As such, identifying variables and mechanisms that can enhance the viability of a long-term study should be given some thought. In other words, it is a good idea to assume the study being implemented will expand and deepen, and therefore laying a foundation for the future is smart. Some specific factors to be concerned with include potential tracking of study participants, combining of administrative data with the assessment battery, using a master list, developmental sensitivities (adolescent-to-adulthood transitions), consistency of measures with respect to the researcher's own scholarly agenda, and funding considerations. There will always be some regrets with respect to the selection of measures, and new insights (and new research questions) from the researcher's own study and findings from other investigators often arise, but the point is to minimize those and be in a position to take advantage of future opportunities.

RACE, ETHNICITY, AND GENDER

Youth of color are overrepresented in the juvenile justice system and the extent of overrepresentation is greater the further into the system that one goes. Although there is considerable debate about the reasons for overrepresentation, it is critical that researchers understand the dynamics of the systems in which they plan to work. Not only is this necessary for purposes such as sampling, training of research staff, and choice of instruments, understanding the flow of cases into the system can also help inform interpretations of results. In addition, there are important gender issues to consider when conducting research in the juvenile justice system. Boys make up more than 70% of cases that are referred to the juvenile court and more than 80% of the youth in juvenile facilities. Yet, the proportion of girls entering the court has increased over the past several decades. Understanding differences in the reasons that girls and boys enter the system, as well as the role that gender and gendered assumptions play in decision making and program development is extremely important in conducting research in the juvenile justice system.

IMPLEMENTATION

It is very important that researchers interested in conducting studies in the juvenile justice system understand the multiple challenges that may be associated with implementation. Although field research in any setting can be challenging, the nature of the juvenile justice system can make research even more challenging. Timing is one challenge that will often arise and researchers should plan very carefully and realize that studies might take longer than if conducted in other settings. For example, getting human subject's approval can take a considerable amount of time and patience given the protections afforded to both kids and prisoners and researchers should plan accordingly. Once human subjects approval is obtained, gathering the necessary consents can be time consuming. Depending on the setting in which the researcher is working, it is not uncommon that events, such as security problems or staffing and cooperation issues, arise that delay data collection. Another hurdle is that contingencies may arise during the course of a study that require that the research design be revised. Although researchers want to adhere to the most rigorous design possible, they must be willing to make changes or develop alternative plans if things such as personnel changes, caseload shifts, or funding allocation changes occur during the course of the study.

Fundamental to successfully implementing a study in a juvenile justice setting is the necessity of building and maintaining relationships. Thus, this is the primary reason why we suggest, and discuss in many of the chapters in this book, that researchers conceptualize projects as partnerships and seek to build the partnership over time. Research projects, although offering some benefits to the entity participating, are also often time and resource intensive. It is likely that the researcher will need to navigate multiple levels of a juvenile justice entity, from the director, judge, or key administrator who gave approval to the staff charged with assisting the researcher. Because members of the staff are likely to have multiple other responsibilities, researchers must work to develop good relationships across these various levels in order to implement the project in a way that does not place burdens on staff. At the same time, given that the research project is likely to be a lower priority than many of the daily tasks of staff and administrators, it is not uncommon for key tasks to get "lost" in these daily activities. Consequently, researchers must play a balancing act between not requesting too much and making sure that tasks get completed.

Based on these challenges, there are a number of practical considerations when implementing research in these settings. Researchers conducting field research in the juvenile justice system should plan on spending a sufficient amount of time in these settings getting to know people and seeking to understand the organizational structure and culture. Researchers must be very careful to build an effective research team due to the sensitivity and intensity of much of the work. Careful planning with regard to the timing of project implementation is another important consideration. For example, some residential institutions might experience turnover at the beginning or start of the school year. Depending on the focus of the study, this might be a time to collect data, or avoid collecting data. Making sure that things are in place—instruments completed, consents obtained, staff trained and ready—during windows of opportunity to collect data is also essential as these windows might close due to events outside of the control of the researcher. Safety and security, be it a court, residential placement, or community program, are also of utmost concern and project staff must be aware of all the rules that are in place and be sensitive to these rules.

It is also important to have a good plan in place for managing and preparing the data for analysis. Often, many projects collect a lot more data than they actually use in preparing reports and publications. Although this cannot be entirely avoided in many cases, having a plan in place for managing data that come in often helps facilitate effective use of the data. Having a good data management plan in place will help to facilitate the use of information and identify areas in which more data need to be collected. It will also help to ensure that data are secured and cannot be accessed by other parties, a requirement in the human subjects process.

HUMAN SUBJECTS IN JUVENILE JUSTICE RESEARCH

The Code of Federal Regulations (45 CFR Part 46) outlines the rules regarding research with human subjects. Subparts C and D concern protections afforded to prisoners and children, respectively. Subpart C prescribes additional duties that IRBs must assume when dealing with studies involving prisoners, addresses the composition of the review board, and lists the type of studies that are permitted with prisoners. Similarly, Subpart D lists the requirements that must be adhered to when conducting research with children including the types of research that can be conducted, requirements regarding the assent of the child, and requirements for the consent of the parents or guardian or the waiver of consent where allowable. Researchers seeking to conduct studies with children who are defined as prisoners must satisfy all the requirements under 45 CFR Part 46, as well as those under both Subparts C and D. Thus, it is very important to become familiar with these requirements prior to planning the study.

The rules provided in these subparts are stringent and mean that gaining approval for research on young people in the juvenile justice system can be very difficult. These requirements are clearly in place to protect these groups, but also present significant challenges to conducting research in juvenile justice settings. Although many IRBs have had experience dealing with studies involving children who are prisoners, these experiences are likely to vary and might require the researcher to help educate the IRB about particular issues and research designs. This is particularly true of studies that employ qualitative or ethnographic methods. Although not as common as other types of study designs, these types of studies can supply valuable depth.

We make two primary suggestions for addressing the various challenges. The first suggestion is to develop relationships with members of the IRB office at your institution. Researchers seeking to gain approval for many types of studies in the juvenile justice system are extremely likely to face full board review at least once if not several times in attempting to gain approval. Developing relationships with IRB staff can help to navigate the rules and requirements, assist throughout the process, and potentially have staff serve as advocates. It can also help keep the researcher abreast of new developments in IRB procedures and rules, including the timing of review meetings and deadlines for the submission of materials. Just as we suggest viewing the research process as a partnership, researchers should view the IRB process, as much as possible, as a partnership and seek to work with the IRB in developing protocols that allow for the research to be conducted but also protect the juveniles, and other individuals, involved in the study.

Our second suggestion is to talk to colleagues, mentors, and other researchers who have conducted similar studies. Because the process can be daunting, and incredibly time consuming, it is helpful to see how other people have navigated the process, designed protocols, developed consent and assent forms, etc. The basic message here is do not, if possible, reinvent the wheel. Researchers have dealt with many similar issues in the past and it is important to draw upon the wisdom of others and to review the various ways that researchers have designed their studies to satisfy human subjects requirements. There may also be individuals in your school or department who can help you make contacts at the IRB to facilitate the process of gaining approval.

As noted previously, human subjects considerations are directly connected to implementation. Not only is it necessary to plan for the time it will take to get approval, researchers should also consider potential issues that might arise after approval. For example, if a study calls for interviews with juveniles, the researcher will need to obtain parental consent (unless they have obtained a waiver). This can be very difficult because it is likely to be dependent on the juvenile justice entity to facilitate the consent process, and, because of the circumstances in which many of these young people live, this may be difficult to obtain. Consequently, researchers should be very cognizant about the feasibility of research projects and designs. Furthermore, the IRB will be very concerned with how data are managed and secured and the implementation plan needs to include concrete steps that will be taken to keep data secure. In addition, researchers working in this area should consider obtaining a Certificate of Confidentiality to provide further protections to participants. We discuss Certificates of Confidentiality in more depth in Chapter 4. It is not impossible to conduct this work, but it does take a great deal of patience and coordination.

BUILDING A RESEARCH TEAM

Many of the types of studies discussed previously require multiple individuals to be involved in the several aspects of the research process. This means that the researcher must build a research team. In doing so, it is necessary to be especially careful given the sensitivity of the issues involved, the rules that govern the system, the experiences that many of the young people in the system have had, and the racial and ethnic composition of the juvenile justice population. It is also important to think about areas of expertise and interest that are needed to conduct the project(s). Many youth involved in the juvenile justice system have mental health or substance abuse problems as well as medical issues, and have experienced trauma, victimization, and discrimination, and a range of other experiences that put them at risk of continual juvenile justice involvement. The complex set of influences that affect these young people often requires that research teams take these factors into account when planning the project.

In addition to being careful in selecting people to work on a project, training is very important. Research team members must be fully aware of the protocol and reasons for the various procedures that are in place. They must understand the setting in which they are working. It is always good to arrange for research team members to see the site and gain an understanding of the rules and regulations in place from staff. If using standardized assessments or instruments, research team members should be provided with the opportunity to conduct mock interviews and work on building a rapport with research participants. The assent and consent procedures should be very clear as well as information on how to handle data once they are collected. The IRB Compliance Office might have tips for administering the protocol and handling information and may be available to meet with the research team prior to beginning the study. We suggest setting up a curriculum of training modules that are directly tied to the research tasks.

DISSEMINATION

There are numerous ways for researchers to disseminate the results of their work—presentations for administrators and staff, technical reports, policy and practice briefs, legislative testimony, Op Eds, presentations at academic and professional meetings and conferences, journal articles, book chapters, and books. A number of other chapters in this book discuss specific academic journals in which research on the juvenile and criminal justice systems can be published (Chapters 3, 4, and 6 in particular). Although these venues are important and researchers should take every opportunity to publish and disseminate their work to the academic community, we also urge researchers to utilize other venues to communicate the key findings of studies. Debates regarding juvenile and criminal justice policy are ongoing and researchers should be engaged in these debates.

In particular, we urge researchers to utilize ways to communicate findings to administrators and staff within the system. Doing so can serve multiple purposes. First, it can help the researcher gather insights from the field that can serve to sharpen interpretations and conclusions. Second, it can help facilitate the partnerships that researchers should be trying to form with actors in the system. Finally, it can reveal findings that are important for administrators and staff to consider and help to lead to new practices and policies. In addition to giving presentations and providing technical reports, we urge researchers to develop other approaches for conveying the findings in a way that is easily discernible to individuals in the field. These approaches can vary considerably, and can be time consuming, but are often quite useful in the field.

CASE STUDY

As discussed previously, cross-sectional studies are fairly efficient and inexpensive research designs that can be used for exploratory, descriptive, and correlational aims. The following case study is an example of a cross-sectional survey that sought to assess the individual, situational, and sociocultural influences on the lives and experiences of incarcerated youth. Knowledge regarding the lives and experiences of young people involved in the juvenile justice system is growing, yet many studies focus on a limited number of influences. The goal of this study was to focus on a range of different influences with the goal of generating research questions and hypotheses that can be tested in subsequent work. Several aspects of this project will be highlighted, including the construction of the instrument, the process of gaining access, the IRB process, and the benefits of the design.

The research design was constructed by three researchers who had significant experience working and doing research in the juvenile justice system and several doctoral students interested in juvenile offenders. These individuals all had different areas of expertise and were able to suggest measures that would provide a multidimensional examination of young offenders. Most of the measures employed in the study were drawn from other work and this required, in some cases, that the researchers obtain permission to use these measures. This was not a problem as there was considerable interest in seeing these measures used in other studies. The research team debated various measures as the goal was to create an instrument that would take approximately 1 hour to administer.

Two private juvenile residential facilities were chosen for the study—one for boys and the other for girls. The facilities were selected in large part because they served a broad range of juvenile offenders and youth were committed to these facilities for a variety of offenses and histories in the juvenile justice system. One of the advantages of working in social work is that many students are working or are in field placements in facilities that serve young people in the juvenile justice system. These students can provide an excellent opportunity for researchers to develop connections in the institutions and access to both of the facilities in this study came through contacts with students. In one instance, the student approached the researchers regarding the interest of the facility in participating in research projects. The other connection came during a visit to check on a student doing her field internship at the institution. The investigators followed up with administrators at both institutions and arranged for the involvement of the two facilities in the study.

Having the facilities express interest in doing research was clearly beneficial to gaining access. Yet, it was also necessary for the researchers to clearly describe the study, its benefits, and the sampling and data collection process in order to gain approval. This took time as final agreement happened over the course of several meetings, emails, and phone calls. It is also important to note that the agreement of the two facilities to be involved did not happen at the same time. The goal of the study was to include both boys and girls so that gender comparisons could be made as a substantial amount of the research on youth in the juvenile justice system has focused mainly on boys. Yet, the budget for the project was small and the investigators knew that logistical and geographic considerations would limit options. Consequently, the design was flexible enough that the researchers knew they could conduct the study with only boys if necessary. In part this is because boys constitute more than 80% of individuals in juvenile residential facilities and the size of the boys facility meant that a sufficient sample size could be obtained to provide meaningful and important findings.

The process of gaining IRB approval started prior to getting agreement from the facilities to conduct research. All IRB protocols require a description and justification of the study and methods and the researchers were able to work on this portion of the protocol while gaining access to the facilities. The IRB process was rocky at the start as the investigators were new to the University and not fully familiar with the process. They reached out to an IRB staff member, but the particular staff member was not entirely familiar with studies involving children who were prisoners. After several meetings and review of protocol drafts, the researchers were referred to another staff member who had more familiarity in this area. This staff member suggested significant changes, further delaying the process. After these changes were made, the initial protocol was submitted to the full board and was returned with substantial modifications. The modifications provided the necessary direction and the protocol was approved upon reconsideration at the subsequent full board meeting.

The protocol required the facilities to contact parents and guardians for consent for a youth to participate in the study and a letter was sent along with a consent form. All materials were approved by the IRB. An assent form was also prepared for the youth to read and sign (consent if over 18 years old). The facility sent out letters to the parents and guardians of sampled youth in waves. Only a limited number, however, were returned. The facility assigned a staff member to contact families, and, although this led to more consents being returned, it did not produce the numbers necessary to complete the study. In making the calls, the staff member concluded that the reason that consents were not being returned was not because parents or guardians did not want their child to participate but because they did not follow through well. According to the facility, this was also the case with other paperwork.

Because the study had been in the field for several months and it was apparent that it would not be successful based on the existing protocol, the researchers considered whether to end the study. A decision, however, was made to approach the IRB and ask about options. Based on discussions with and the help of a colleague, the researchers requested a meeting with the IRB Director. At the meeting, one of the researchers explained the situation and an alternative plan was developed. The IRB Director determined that the researchers had complied with all of the requirements but that it was not feasible to complete the study using the current protocol. Therefore, the researchers should request a waiver of parental consent. This required a substantial revision of the protocol, in part because the University had moved from paper submissions to an online process. The protocol was submitted to the full board and returned with substantial changes. Because some of these changes contradicted what the IRB required in the first protocol, the researchers contacted the Director for clarification and assistance. The Director reviewed the protocol prior to its resubmission and indicated his support to the board.

The protocol was approved and the data collection process began. The time period during which the request for parental waiver was being considered allowed for the researchers to modify the instrument somewhat based on the initial data collection efforts. This led to the introduction of several different sets of questions. Prior to beginning the data collection process, interviewers attended a training session and conducted mock interviews. The training session included a description of the study, including its design, and protocol. Materials were provided to each interviewer.

Data collection occurred over a period of 7–8 months. The boys facility was an hour away from campus and the plan was to use the summer to make weekly trips. A team of between three and five individuals went up on each trip and each individual was able to interview two or three youth each day. The facility allowed the researchers to use the visiting center for interviews because it was empty during the periods that the researchers were at the facility. It offered sufficient space and privacy for the interviews. The summer provided sufficient time to conduct the interviews at the boys facility. The girls facility was very close to campus so data were collected during the fall and winter by a smaller group of interviewers.

Data collection occurred through the use of computers whereby data were directly placed in a file that could be readily transferred to a standard statistical software package for analysis. The investigators contracted with an individual who was experienced with the necessary technology to help set up the database and train a doctoral student on how to use the technology. This was cost efficient because it utilized someone with experience to set up the program but then enabled someone from the research team to complete the process, make necessary changes, and manage the data. Once data collection was complete, the data were transferred to statistical programs. The research team worked together to clean the data and organize the data file. Individuals with expertise working with different measures were charged with constructing necessary variables and syntax was created for each step. For security purposes, the data are controlled by the investigators. The data are now being analyzed and analyses are being conducted by the investigators with students and colleagues interested in specific research questions. One paper has been published, several more are underway, and initial analyses are already leading to the development of additional research questions.

CONCLUSIONS

There are many opportunities for social work researchers to conduct research in the juvenile justice system. This work has substantial challenges, but these challenges can be overcome. To do so, researchers need to be realistic about what they would like to do, cognizant of the need to build relationships, and very purposeful in their planning. We highly encourage researchers to become involved in the juvenile justice system because it affects a substantial number of children and juvenile justice policy and practice are a matter of significant debate.

ADDITIONAL READING

Grisso, T., Vincent, G., & Seagrave, D. (2005). *Mental health screening and assessment in juvenile justice.* New York: Guilford Press.

This edited volume provides an overview of numerous mental health screening tools that can be usefully employed by researchers in juvenile justice settings.

Howell, J. C. (2009). *Preventing and reducing juvenile delinquency: A comprehensive framework–second edition.* Thousand Oaks, CA: Sage Publications.

A well-rounded text on many issues relevant to conducting research in juvenile justice settings including an examination of the research base on trends in juvenile offending, gangs, and programmatic and prevention issues.

2

Using Extant Research on Juveniles

INTRODUCTION

Numerous data sets have accrued based on research funded by myriad agencies, federal and nonfederal, and private foundations. In contrast to administrative data, these data sources are commonly designed and collected by university-based scholars and range in scope from local cross-sectional studies to national surveys and large-scale long-term longitudinal research. As such, these data sets represent a rich resource for tackling a wide variety of research questions on juveniles. Some of the many advantages of using shared extant data have been identified. For example, Fienberg (1994) notes that data-sharing facilitates open scientific inquiry, provide diverse views based on various analyses, increase debate with respect to important constructs and findings across data sets, and promote new research. Shared extant data also are efficient. Several data files have produced hundreds and perhaps thousands of reports. Many large data collection efforts have cost the tax payers millions of dollars and researchers and study participants have given their time to these projects and it is arguably unethical to waste these data.

This chapter will describe the advantages and disadvantages of using extant research data sources on juveniles, suggest techniques to surmount common problems encountered when using these data sets, illustrate the types of data that are commonly available, show readers how to access and analyze these data, and provide guidance on dissemination and publication based on these types of data. To further enhance the execution of using extant research data an annotated bibliography of available data files and additional readings is presented.

GETTING STARTED: TYPES OF STUDY DATA COMMONLY AVAILABLE

There are many types of data that are available for research on juveniles. These include data on juvenile offender or incarcerated youth populations and data on adolescents and youth in general. One might ask why include data on youth in general? The answer is that many of these large data files contain information on arrests, past delinquent behavior, and contact with the juvenile justice system. Although many data sets have this information, they often go unanalyzed because they were not the primary intent of the project and the title of the project does not suggest these types of variables are included. For example, the National Survey on Drug Use and Health (NSDUH) has a youth experiences question section for 12- to 17-year-old study participants that contains items on handgun carrying, drug selling, and other delinquent behavior.

Extant data sources have been collected using a wide variety of research designs ranging from cross-sectional surveys (including complex sampling—more on this in Chapter 6) to multiwave longitudinal investigations. Fewer data based on experimental designs are available. This is because relative to other designs, experimental designs are expensive and social science researchers are often not trained in experimental methods or undervalue these approaches perhaps due to their applied nature and implementation difficulties. Thus, fewer experimental studies are conducted. Most of the data collections are funded by federal (e.g., National Institutes of Health) and foundational (e.g., MacArthur Foundation) sources. One might wonder why the National Institute of Justice (NIJ) is not a leading funder of research on juveniles. NIJ relative to other federal sources of funding has a very small budget for research.

For example, justice-related research accounts for less than 1% of the budget allotted for health-related research (Clear, 2009; Petersilia, 1991; see also Welsh & Farrington, 2007).

One question that often comes up pertains to the age of the data itself. Although newer or current data are preferred, older extant data can still be employed to answer important questions (e.g., promotive factors for desistance from delinquency). Using older data may require more time spent providing a rationale for their use because article reviewers may frown on the use of older data sources that are not up to date with respect to a given phenomenon.

SOURCES OF RESEARCH DATA ON JUVENILES

The largest repository of extant research data including qualitative data sources is housed in the Inter-University Consortium for Political and Social research (ICPSR) at the University of Michigan. The stated mission of ICPSR is to "provide leadership and training in data access, curation, and methods of analysis for a diverse and expanding social science research community." ICPSR has a data archive of over 500,000 data files pertaining to disciplines such as criminal justice, political science, gerontology, public health, psychology, education, and racial and ethnic minorities. More than 500 data files are added to ICPSR each year (http://www.icpsr.umich.edu/icpsrweb/ICPSR/access/index.jsp). It should also be noted that much of these data is cross-listed on other sites such as the University of California at Los Angeles Social Science Data Archive (http://www.sscnet.ucla.edu/issr/da/Home.WhatsNew.htm).

Many data sets have not been deposited at ICPSR but can be obtained for analysis by contacting the principal investigator (PI) of an ongoing study. For example, Rolf Loeber, PI of the Pittsburgh Youth Study—a longitudinal investigation that has yielded insights into the development of problem behavior over the life-course, is open to researchers outside of the project proposing analyses to answer specific research questions. Although PIs vary greatly in their willingness to share data, most PIs are open to reasonable proposals for research explorations of the data they have collected. Certainly, most study leaders will not simply "hand over" data for analysis. There are several reasons for this. First, these researchers have spent considerable portions of their professional careers in collecting these data and are justifiably guarded about releasing data (not to mention potential internal review board issues). This is not a result of selfishness but more of a concern that data will be thoughtfully analyzed using correct statistical procedures that attempt to answer a research question that makes a genuine contribution to the literature. Taking the time to develop a relationship with a PI of an ongoing study and developing a productive research question are key steps in executing a competent analysis that leads to a peer-reviewed article. To effectively do so, it is necessary to take the time to read and become familiar with the design, measures, and articles that have been published using the data. Some data repositories provide links to much of this information.

ACCESSING THE DATA

Data can be accessed via multiple sources, including, but not limited to, federal and state government websites, organizational websites, academic journals and colleagues, etc. However, it is advised to first begin a search using the ICPSR data because of its large number of data files, and because it is a "clearing house," of sorts, for other previously mentioned sources.

The following is a step-by-step description of how to access a data file on the ICPSR website.

1. Go to http://www.icpsr.umich.edu/icpsrweb/ICPSR/
2. Under the drop down menu entitled "Find & Analyze Data," click on "Find ICPSR Data."
3. There will be a blank field next to a "Search for Data" button.
4. Type your keywords into the blank field and click on the "Search for Data" button. (Note: The search can also be done at the ICPSR home page in the blank field at the top right of the page. However, you must make sure that the "Search for Data" button is filled or populated.)

5. Once you type your keyword(s) and have clicked on the "Search for Data" button, the ICPSR website will present all relevant data for that keyword. You can sort the data alphabetically, by title, its release date, by time period, and by the categories of "most downloaded" and "most cited in ICPSR bib." (This is done by using the drop down menu located at the top of the search results page.)

6. In reviewing the list of data sets presented during the initial search query, choose those that sound pertinent to your research query and click on its hyperlink. Upon doing so, the ICPSR website takes the researcher to a descriptive page for the data. This page offers a download link for the data (the download button will notify the researcher in what forms (documentation only, SAS, SPSS, or Stata) the data exist, a summary of the data file you have chosen, access notes regarding any information that may be restricted to the researcher, and a description of where the data set is maintained and distributed. The page also offers the reader an explanation of what the data set can be used for. A thorough review of this page is pertinent for understanding the possible benefits of the data for a particular research interest.

DATA MANIPULATION

Usually, the data that are downloaded will be formatted in a commonly used statistical software package such as SPSS (now PASW), SAS, or Stata. Because universities often support particular software, not every researcher or student will have the software that the data file is in. This can easily be surmounted by using statTransfer software (available from circle systems, www.stattransfer.com), a program that allows data to be transferred between different data analysis packages including very specialized software.

Once you have downloaded the data file and can open it in a data analysis package that you use there are numerous manipulations that you will have to do depending on your research question or aims.

Fortunately, many publicly available data files have been cleaned with scales summed and are accompanied by a useful codebook that indicates the variables that are available in the data file. In fact, most repositories such as ICPSR have clear guidelines for data deposits and a process policy in place toward achieving the goal of independent use of the data. What does this process look like? Figure 2.1 graphically depicts the data deposit to access process. See http://www.icpsr.umich.edu/icpsrweb/ICPSR/access/deposit/pipeline.jsp.

Many researchers, however, will wish to create variables for their own specific uses. Prior to new variable creation, running frequency procedures to examine patterns in the study variables that are of interest is important. Every seasoned data analyst realizes that there is no substitute for getting to know your data at a descriptive level including information not typically available in the codebook or questionnaire such as variable departures from normality (e.g., skewness). However, there is disagreement about the precise level of skewness that can be tolerated with values above the range of 0.8–1.0 considered to reflect a need for transformation (square root or log transformed usually suffice). Some variables are so badly skewed they need to be treated as categories. One common

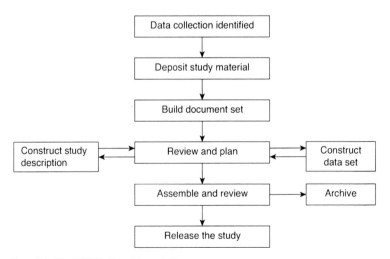

Figure 2.1. The ICPSR Data Deposit Process.

departure from normality seen in criminal and juvenile justice research involves variables that are measured as counts. Counts are variables where many in the sample will have a zero score. For example, if your dependent variable is number of motor vehicle thefts many youth in juvenile justice settings may have not committed this crime, yet the range on the count variable can be from 0 to 50—a distribution that statisticians characterize as a Poisson distribution. The variable could be categorized as none, few, moderate, many etc., but this type of overdispersion in the data is often handled by means of a negative binomial regression or related Poisson-type regression model (e.g., Lattimore, MacDonald, Piquero, Linster, & Visher, 2004). Although more accurate in a statistical sense, these types of models are not always easily interpretable.

RESEARCHING PRIOR USES OF THE DATA

When embarking on a program of research using an extant data file it is a good idea to find out what has been previously explored in the data. One obvious reason for doing this is you do not want to repeat what has already been done. Another important reason is that by reading previously published articles that have used these data you gain insight into how other researchers have used the data including measures and various analytic strategies. New ideas and gaps that can be addressed in future papers are often identified by reading these reports. Many data sets are associated with large projects that have their own websites and maintain a bibliography that makes it fairly easy to examine what has been published using the data file. When such a listing is not readily available then focusing on key authors that were the principal investigators of the project is usually a good strategy. Various search engines such as PsycINFO, Medline or PubMed, Social Science Abstracts, Criminal Justice Abstracts, abstracts of the National Criminal Justice Reference Service, and even Google Scholar are useful to track down articles by a specific author. Once you have done this then examining the reference sections of identified articles to find more publications using the data file can be conducted.

DATA ANALYTIC CONSIDERATIONS AND STRATEGIES

Depending on the nature of the research question there are a wide variety of statistical methods that can be employed with extant data sources on juveniles. One of the first things to understand about an extant data source is the sampling frame. The sampling frame specifies the procedures used to collect the data from a pool of participants. Sampling frames vary widely. For example, a cross-sectional study of incarcerated adolescents at one facility is very different in its sampling frame from a nationally representative study of juvenile offenders, with the latter being far more complex and layered. The reason why this is important is that the design of the sampling frame has to be taken into account when analyzing the data in order to avoid biased estimates. Table 2.1 provides a number of useful questions that should be answered by a researcher when conducting an analysis and reporting the results. As can be readily seen, optimal data analysis is systematic in nature. Following guidelines listed below not only facilitates a stronger analysis but also provides a fuller understanding of the data for the reader.

Table 2.1. A General Data Analytic Checklist.

✓ Are the goals, aims, or research questions/hypotheses clearly stated?
✓ Is the sampling frame clearly defined and presented?
✓ Is the sample clearly described?
✓ Is relevant psychometric information (reliability and validity of measures) presented?
✓ Are the variables to be used in the analysis made explicit (i.e., dependent, independent, and control) and operationalized?
✓ Are the fundamental distributional properties (measurement, mean, variability, skewness, and kurtosis) of the study variables assessed?
✓ Are missing data dealt with?
✓ Are the assumptions underlying the analyses met?
✓ Are the name and version of software used reported?
✓ Are the estimation problems documented?
✓ Are effect sizes (r, odds ratio, Cohen's d) and not p-values guiding the narration of results, especially in large samples?
✓ Are causal statements avoided unless the research design facilitates?

Adapted from Hancock, G. R., & Miller, R. O. (2010). *The reviewer's guide to quantitative methods in the social sciences.* New York: Routledge Press.

DISSEMINATION

No matter how well a study of extant data is conducted if no one reads the study, it is of little use. Thus, the issue of dissemination is critically important (see Chapter 6 for an extended discussion of the issue). Although peer-reviewed journals are a primary source of data for the community of scholars, other ways to disseminate information such as secondary digests of information, editorials, policy, and technical reports can be very useful depending on the target audience. A common question that arises is whether study results disseminated as a peer-reviewed journal article can also be revised in a different form to inform a different audience such as policy-makers. The answer is yes as long as there are no copyright violations and appropriate acknowledgments are employed.

Although with respect to research on juveniles there is a plethora of journal outlets that can be considered for publications, researchers should carefully consider the focus of the journal and its primary readership. In addition, researchers should weigh their career trajectory relative to where they would like to see their scholarship appear vis-à-vis their career goals. Table 2.2 displays a number of journals that can be considered for work on adolescent problem behavior and juvenile justice samples. Although we list the journal impact factor, which is the averaged number of times an article is cited in a journal over a 2-year period of time, impact factors change over time, though often not dramatically.

DISADVANTAGES OF USING EXTANT RESEARCH DATA

Although possessing numerous advantages, using extant research data is not without any disadvantages. One of the major disadvantages of using extant data is that you are limited to what already exists. By not having any control over the data collection some extant data will not have many of the variables that a researcher is interested in most. Typically, there are measures a researcher wished were in the data file. Another limitation is

Table 2.2. A Sample of Journal Outlets for Research on Juveniles

Adolescent Journals	Impact Factor*
Journal of Adolescence	1.80
Journal of Research in Adolescence	1.68
Journal of Adolescent Research	1.40
Journal of Youth and Adolescence	1.38
Journal of Early Adolescence	1.27
Adolescence	0.79
Criminology/Criminal Justice Journals	
Criminology	2.63
Law and Human Behavior	2.62
Journal of Research in Crime and Delinquency	2.03
Criminal Justice and Behavior	1.69
Crime and Delinquency	1.54
Justice Quarterly	1.18
Youth Violence and Juvenile Justice	0.85**
Journal of Criminal Justice	0.80

*Based on year 2009 data.
**Recent journal—alternative impact factor used.

the data may also be old and have utilized measures that are somewhat out of date. Using extant data files may be seductive but could take researchers away from collecting data that they really are interested in. In addition, there is much to be learned by implementing a field design and collecting your own data. Moving from dissertation to a career trajectory of relying solely on extant data analysis can be constraining in terms of overall growth as a researcher. Being involved in multiple research designs and employing various forms of data, including extant data, are often rewarding and provide numerous insights into a phenomenon of interest.

CONCLUSIONS

Using extant data files to study juveniles represents a rich and powerful source of information. These data files are easily obtainable or can be obtained by request. Although researchers frequently use these sources, much of the data goes unused. A wide variety of sources exist and taking time to explore variables contained in these diverse data sets via codebooks and questionnaires can lead to fruitful discoveries. Furthermore, these forays will often catalyze new ideas for future data collections.

ADDITIONAL READINGS

Boslaugh, S. (2007). *Secondary data sources for public health: A practical guide.* New York: Cambridge University Press.

Smith, E. (2008). *Using secondary data in educational and social research.* New York: McGraw-Hill.

Trzesniewski, K. H., Donnellan, M. B., & Lucas, R. E. (2010). *Secondary data analysis: An introduction for psychologists.* Washington, DC: American Psychological Association.

ANNOTATED BIBLIOGRAPHY OF DATA SOURCES

Described below is a large number, yet not exhaustive list, of extant data sets that can be used to examine research questions on juveniles. Most of these are publicly available and relatively easy to obtain. However, some data files listed are not available through ICPSR. Because new data sets are continually being added researchers should explore ICPSR to identify data sets for their specific needs.

Project on Human Development in Chicago Neighborhoods (PHDCN) Series, 1995–2002

Sample Size/Population: Chicago residents comprising 8782 adults and over, plus 6000 children, adolescents, and young adults

Time: 1995–2002

Assessments: Two surveys using systematic social observation (SSO) techniques were done on 343 Chicago neighborhood blocks (n = 8782 adults), as well two longitudinal studies (Infant Assessment Unit and Longitudinal Cohort Study; n = 6,000 children, adolescents and young adults). The longitudinal studies examined subjects' lives and their shifting environmental conditions in regard to antisocial behaviors.

Health Behavior in School-Aged Children (HBSC)
   Sample Size/Population: Varies/chool-aged children from the United States
   Time: 2001–2002 for United States
   Assessments: The data available at ICPSR are from the results of the United States survey conducted during the 2001–2002 school year. The study contains variables dealing with many types of drugs such as tobacco, alcohol, marijuana, inhalants, and any other substances and examines the first time these substances were used, as well as the frequency of their use.

National Health Interview Survey (NHIS), Youth Risk Behavior (YRB) Survey, and YRB Supplement Survey
   Sample Size/Population: Varies/American youth
   Time: 1992–Present (on-going)
   Assessments: The Youth Risk Behavior Survey monitors the major risk behaviors of American youth, including gender, age, race, marital status, veteran status, education, income, industry and occupation codes, and limits on activity. Unique variables include questions on topics such as injury risks, weapons use, alcohol and drug use, cigarette smoking, diet/nutrition, and sexual behaviors, among others.

Monitoring the Future: A Continuing Study of American Youth
   Sample Size/Population: Varies/American youth
   Time: 2009 (most recent)
   Assessments: This is part of a series exploring topics such as values, behaviors, and lifestyle orientations of contemporary American youth. Questionnaires within the study contained "core" questions related to demographics and drug use. Other topics on the questionnaire included violence/crime (both in and out of school), self-esteem, religion,

changing roles for women, educational aspirations, and exposure to drug education.

National Youth Survey, Waves 1–7

Sample Size/Population: Representative sample of young people in the United States

Time: Wave 1 (1976), Wave 2 (1977), Wave 3 (1978), Wave 4 (1979), Wave 5 (1980), Wave 6 (1983), Wave 7 (1987)

Assessments: The study attempted to gain a better understanding of the conventional and deviant types of behavior by youths.

Annual Survey of Jails in Indian Country Series

Sample Size/Population: Adults and juveniles in Indian reservations, pueblos, Rancherias, and other Native American and Alaska Native communities throughout the United States

Time: 1998 to present

Assessments: The survey provides data on inmates, staffing, and facility characteristics, as well as the needs of all confinement facilities operated by tribal authorities or the Bureau of Indian Affairs (BIA).

Annual Survey of Jails

Sample Size/Population: Adult and juvenile U.S. inmate populations

Time: 1982 to present

Assessments: Every 5 to 6 years, census data on the full size of the jail population and selected inmate characteristics are obtained.

Arrestee Drug Abuse Monitoring (ADAM) Program/Drug Use
Forecasting (DUF) Series

Sample Size/Population: 1987–1997 included 24 sites across the United States from U.S. criminals arrested and booked (number of sites varied from year to year). Juvenile data were added in 1991. In 2000, the sites were increased to 35 cities, only looking at adult populations of arrestees. Note: The data represent only the number of arrests, as opposed to an unduplicated count of persons arrested.

Time: 1987–1997, 2000–present

Assessments: The DUF program was designed to estimate the prevalence of drug use and detect changes in trends in drug use among U.S.

persons arrested and booked. Arrestees supplied self-report measures and urine samples. (Urine samples were screened for 10 illicit drugs.) Note: In 2000, the ADAM program, redesigned from the DUF program, moved to a probability-based sampling for only the adult male population.

Census of Public and Private Juvenile Detention, Correctional, and Shelter Facilities Series

Sample Size/Population: Public and private juvenile facilities in the United States, including residential programs and group homes (only those housing three or more residents, with 50% of the residents being juveniles, and having a daily average of 1% of accused or adjudicated delinquents and status offenders)

Time: 1984–1985 (public facilities only); 1986–1987 and beyond (both pubic and private facilities)

Assessments: This data provide information on population characteristics within juvenile facilities within the United States. Note: Excluded from the data were juvenile facilities operated as part of adult jails, non-residential facilities, facilities exclusively for drug or alcohol abusers or nonoffenders, and federal juvenile correctional facilities.

Census of State and Federal Adult Correctional Facilities Series

Sample Size/Population: Federal and state-operated adult confinement and correctional facilities within the United States, including youthful offender facilities (except in California)

Time: Ongoing; produced every 5 years

Assessments: Data variables include, but are not limited to, physical security, capital and operating expenditures, custody level of residents/inmates, race/ethnicity of inmates, inmate deaths, and assaults and incidents by inmates.

Juvenile Court Statistics Survey

Sample Size/Population: Juvenile cases disposed by courts with jurisdiction over juvenile matters

Time: 1926 to present

Assessments: This survey encompasses extensive detailed information on youth who come in contact with the juvenile justice system, as well as on the activities of the nation's juvenile courts.

National Crime Victimization Survey (NCVS) Series
Sample Size/Population: Cluster samples of U.S. victims, 12 and older
Time: Ongoing
Assessments: NCVS gives detailed information about the victims and consequences of crime, estimates the number and classification of crimes not reported to police, and provides measures of selected types of crime.

National Health and Nutritional Examination Survey (NHANES) and Follow-up Series
Sample Size/Population: Cluster samples of civilian noninstitutionalized U.S. residents with high risks for malnutrition, ages 2 months to 74 years.
Time: 1959–1984 (Four-Part Series)
Assessments: The NHANES I Epidemiologic Follow-up Study (NHEFS) is a longitudinal study designed to investigate the relationships between clinical, nutritional, and behavioral factors. NHANES II (1976–1980) was designed to continue the measurement and monitoring of the nutritional status and health of the U.S. population. NHANES III (1988–1994) contains information on a sample of 33,994 persons aged 2 months and older. The Hispanic HANES (HHANES) was conducted to obtain sufficient numbers to produce estimates of the health and nutritional status of Hispanics, as well as specific data for Puerto Ricans, Mexican-Americans, and Cuban-Americans.

National Jail Census Series
Sample Size/Population: U.S. jail population, both juvenile and adult (excludes federal and/or state administered facilities, as well as jail-prison systems in Alaska, Connecticut, Delaware, Hawaii, Rhode Island, and Vermont)
Time: Every 5 Years (most recent 2006)
Assessments: Data include jail population by reason being held, age and sex, etc.

National Longitudinal Surveys (NLS) Series
Sample Size/Population: Five groups of Americans: older men aged 45–59, mature women aged 30–44, young men aged 14–24, young

women aged 14–24, and youths aged 14–21. Children born to mothers within the survey

Time: 1960s to present (youth: 1979 to present); (children: 1986 to present)

Assessments: A set of longitudinal surveys relating to the labor market experiences of five specific groups of American men and women. The data also include cognitive-socioemotional-physiological assessments administered to NLSY mothers and their children. Note: The Bureau of Labor Statistics website contains the most current data for this series.

National Survey on Drug Use and Health

Sample Size/Population: Within this annual survey is a categorical variable that selects the 12- to 17-year-old group (N = 17,842, 2008 survey).

Time: Annual survey

Assessments: Extensive alcohol, drug, and tobacco use questions. In addition to sociodemographics, there are items that assess delinquent behaviors, parental involvement, and school and treatment experiences.

National Youth Survey (NYS) Series

Sample Size/Population: U.S. parents and youth

Time: Conducted in 7 Waves (Wave 1, 1976) and (Wave 7, 1987)

Assessments: Questions pertaining to events and behaviors of the preceding year were asked in order to gain an understanding of both conventional and deviant types of behavior by youths. Data include the demographic and socioeconomic status of respondents, disruptive events in the home, neighborhood problems, labeling, parental discipline, community involvement, drug and alcohol use, victimization, pregnancy, depression, etc.

State Court Statistics Series

Sample Size/Population: State appellate and Trial Court caseloads by type of case for the 50 states, District of Columbia, and Puerto Rico

Time: Ongoing annually

Assessments: Major areas of investigation include case filings, case dispositions, and appellate opinions. Case types include civil cases, capital punishment cases, other criminal cases, juvenile cases, administrative agency appeals, and several other types.

Uniform Crime Reporting Program Data [United States] Series
Sample Size/Population: Reported crimes not available elsewhere in the criminal justice system
Time: 1929–present
Assessments: ICPSR archives the UCR data as five separate components: summary data, county-level data, incident-level data, hate crime data, and various, mostly nonrecurring, data collections.

Youth Studies Series
Sample Size/Population: Biologically related generations of high school seniors and their parents across time
Time: 1965, 1973, 1982, 1997
Assessments: The objective was to study the dynamics of political attitudes and behaviors by obtaining data on the same individuals as they aged from approximately 18 years in 1965 to 50 years in 1997. Analysis of generational, life cycle, and historical effects and political influences on relationships within the family can be discerned.

Other Sources

Juvenile Justice Data Project
Sample Size/Population: 50 county probation departments in California reported on juvenile populations, with 95% of the youth aged 19 and older
Time: 2004
Assessments: Self-report measures on juvenile statistics were administered to 58 county probation departments in California. Data on early intervention, regular supervision, intensive supervision, county aftercare, placement, court-ordered commitment, and state confinement and parole were gathered.

Juvenile Violence Research from the Office of Juvenile Justice and Delinquency Prevention (OJJDP)
Sample Size/Population: American juveniles
Time: 1992 to present
Assessments: A compendium of research from the OJJDP, which includes data on identifying characteristics/patterns of at-risk juveniles

and the factors contributing to such violence, data on the accessibility of firearms and their use by or against juveniles, and data on conditions associated with an increase in violence among the juvenile population. Several other violence studies under OJJDP include the following:

A. **Studies of Violence Committed by or against juveniles in Washington, DC**—Looked at 2686 juveniles aged 12 to 17 years charged with violent offenses in 1993–1995 in Washington, DC, 128 juvenile homicide victimizations in 1993–1995, and 2971 juvenile violent victimizations in 1993–1994.

B. **Juvenile Violence in Los Angeles, CA**—Special emphasis placed on gang violence; the study looked at a random sample of 311 homicide incidents involving 12- to 17-year-old males in 1993 and 1994 from three jurisdiction in LA. The survey consisted of 349 males ages 12 to 17 randomly sampled from eight high-crime LA county neighborhoods.

C. **Violence Among Rural Youth** (1994–present)—Data included homicides committed by juveniles, patterns of gun ownership among middle school students (the sample size was 6263 students in 36 middle schools during 1996), bullying and antisocial behavior among middle school students (survey of 6389 fourth-, fifth-, and sixth-grade students from six rural school districts in South Carolina conducted in 1995), bullying prevention, and community factors affecting violence among rural youth.

D. **The Milwaukee Homicide Study**—Homicides involving juveniles in Milwaukee in 1992 and 1993. The study included adolescent (13–17 years old) and young adult offenders (18–24 years old); interviews were conducted with 86 offenders and 57 next of kin of homicide victims.

Three longitudinal projects initiated in 1986 include the following:

A. **Denver Youth Survey:** A longitudinal multidisciplinary study of developmental patterns consisting of 1527 Denver males and females age 7, 9, 11 13, and 15 years in 1988.

B. **Pittsburgh Youth Study:** Progressions in Antisocial and Delinquent Child Behavior. The study consists of a random sample of 1517 males in first, fourth, and seventh grades in 1987 in Pittsburgh public schools.
C. **Rochester Youth Development Study:** A panel study of a reciprocal Causal Model of Delinquency. This ongoing study consists of a random sample of 1000 males and females from Development Study seventh and eighth graders in 1987 from Rochester public schools.

The MacArthur Juvenile Adjudicative Competence Study
Sample Size/Population: 1400 males between the ages of 11 and 24 years in Philadelphia, Los Angeles, Northern and Eastern Virginia, and Northern Florida; 50% of those males were in jail or detained in a juvenile correction facility
Time: 2003
Assessments: These tests assessed their competence to stand trial, their legal decision making in several hypothetical scenarios, intelligence, mental health problems, and prior experience in the justice system.

The National Juvenile Court Data Archive
Sample Size/Population: More than 800,000 juvenile court cases containing 67% of the juvenile population
Time: 1927 to present
Assessments: Juvenile and family courts across the country provide demographic information about juveniles involved in delinquency, reasons for the juveniles referral to court, and the court's response to the juvenile delinquency.

Children's Defense Fund (CDF) State of America's Children 2010 Report (www.childrensdefensefund.org)
Sample Size/Population: U.S. children
Time: 2010
Assessments: Compilation of data taken from national and state data on poverty, health, child welfare, youth at-risk, education, early childhood development, nutrition, gun violence, and housing.

National Longitudinal Study of Adolescent Health (Add Health)

Sample Size/Population: Nationally representative sample of approximately 15,000–20,000 adolescents enrolled in grades 7 through 12 from 130 middle/high schools across the country

Time: Waves 1–2, 1994–1996; Wave 3, 2001–2002; Wave 4, 2007–2009

Assessments: Four waves of data were collected; Wave 1 in-home component was composed of interviews with 20,745 adolescents and 17,700 of their primary caregivers. Wave 2, 14,738 youths were asked questions pertaining to their social relationships, behaviors, and school experiences; Wave 3 included questions pertaining to 15,197 young adults, such as marital status, employment history, and childbearing status. Wave 4 included personal interviews, physical measurements, and biospecimen collection.

Haapanen and Steiner's (2006) California Youth Authority Study

Sample Size/Population: 813 serious juvenile delinquents committed to the CYA between 1997 and 1999

Time: 1997–1999

Assessments: Self-report assessments on mental health problems among institutionalized delinquents.

Oregon Research Institute

Sample Size/Population: Oregon children and adolescents

Time: 1960 to present

Assessments: Behavioral problems in children, teen substance abuse, adolescent depression, and other social problems.

Cambridge Study in Delinquent Development (David P. Farrington and Donald J. West)

Sample Size/Population: Longitudinal study starting with 411 boys at age 8 from a working-class area of London with follow-ups to age 32

Time: 1961 to 1985

Assessments: The survey was used to describe delinquent and criminal behavior among inner-city males, prediction of such behavior, why juvenile delinquency begins and continues or does not continue into adulthood, and why crime ends when the men reached their 20s or 30s.

Adoption and Twin Studies

(See Soo Hyun Rhee and Irwin D. Waldman, "Genetic and
Environmental Influences on Antisocial Behavior:
A Meta-Analysis of Twin and Adoption Studies.")

a. Texas Adoptees
   Studies: Loehlin et al. (1985, 1987)
   Assessments: Psychopathy

b. St. Louis Adoptees
   Studies: Cadoret et al. (1975) and Cunningham et al. (1975)
   Assessments: Antisocial Behavior

c. Dutch Adoptees
   Studies: van den Oord et al. (1994)
   Assessments: Antisocial Behaviors

d. U.S. adoptees (CO, IL, MN, WI)
   Studies: McGue et al. (1996)
   Assessments: Antisocial Behaviors

e. Iowa Adoptees
   Studies: Cadoret et al. (1978, 1985–1987, 1990–1991)
   Assessments: Antisocial behaviors, conduct disorder (CD), antisocial personality, and criminality

f. Danish Adoptees
   Studies: Hutchings and Mednick (1971), Mednick et al. (1983), Gabrielli and Mednick (1984), Baker (1986), Baker et al. (1989)
   Assessments: Criminality

g. Swedish Adoptees
   Studies: Bohman (1978), Bohman et al. (1982), and Sigvardsson et al. (1982)
   Assessments: Criminality

h. Colorado Adoptees
   Studies: Deater-Deckard and Plomin (1999), Young et al. (1997, personal communication), Young et al. (1996, personal communication), Parker et al. (1989, as cited in Carey, 1994)
   Assessments: Aggression, delinquency, and conduct disorder

i. Midwest Twins
   Studies: Cates et al. (1993)
   Assessments: Aggression

j. National Academy of Sciences/National Research Council Twins
   Studies: Centerwall and Robinette (1989), Horn et al. (1976)
   Assessments: Criminality and psychopathy

k. California Twins
   Studies: Ghodsian-Carpey and Baker (1978)
   Assessments: Aggression

l. Danish Twins
   Studies: Carey (1992), Christiansen (1973, 1974, 1977a), and Cloninger et al. (1978)
   Assessments: Criminality

m. London Twins
   Studies: Stevenson and Graham (1988), Wilson et al. (1977), Rushton et al. (1986), and Rushton (1996)
   Assessments: Antisocial behaviors, aggression, delinquency, and violence

n. Minnesota Twins (reared apart)
   Studies: DiLalla et al. (1996), Grove et al. (1990), Bouchard and McGue (1990), Gottesman et al. (1984), Tellegen et al. (1988)
   Assessments: Psychopathy, adult antisocial personality (ASP), child ASP, and aggression

o. Minnesota Twins (reared together)
   Studies: Tellegen et al. (1988), Lykken et al. (1978), McGue et al. (1993)
   Assessments: Aggression

p. Minnesota Twins (adolescents)
   Studies: Taylor et al. (2000), Hershberger et al. (1995)
   Assessments: Psychopathy, delinquency, and CD

q. Minnesota Twins (adults)
   Studies: Finkel and McGue (1997)
   Assessments: Aggression

r. Boston Twins (adolescents)
   Studies: Gottesman (1965, 1966)
   Assessments: Psychopathy

s. Boston Twins (children)
   Studies: Scarr (1966)
   Assessments: Aggression

t. Vancouver Twins
   Studies: Livesley et al. (1993)
   Assessments: Antisocial behaviors

u. National Merit Scholarship Twins
   Studies: Loehlin and Nichols (1976)
   Assessments: Pyschopathy

v. Calgary Twins
   Studies: Lytton et al. (1988)
   Assessments: Antisocial behaviors

w. Philadelphia Twins
   Studies: Meininger et al. (1988)
   Assessments: Aggression

x. Missouri Twins
   Studies: Owen and Sines (1970)
   Assessments: Aggression

y. Colorado Twins
   Studies: O'Connor et al. (1980), Plomin and Foch (1980), Plomin (1981), Zahn-Waxler et al. (1996), Schmitz et al. (1994, 1995), Wilcutt et al. (1995)
   Assessments: Aggression, antisocial behaviors, and conduct problems

z. Ohio Twins
   Studies: Rowe (1983)
   Assessments: Antisocial behaviors

aa. Norwegian Twins
   Studies: Torgersen et al. (1993)
   Assessments: Psychopathy

bb. California Twins
   Studies: Rahe et al. (1978)
   Assessments: Aggression

cc. Virginia Twins
   Studies: Eaves et al. (1978), Silberg et al. (1994, 1996), Simonoff et al. (1995)
   Assessments: Antisocial behaviors, aggression, and conduct problems

dd. Indiana Twins
   Studies: Pogue-Geile and Rose (1985), Brandon and Rose (1995), Rose (1988)
   Assessments: Psychopathy

ee. British Columbia Twins
   Studies: Blanchard et al. (1995)
   Assessments: Aggression

ff. Australian Twins (children)
   Studies: Waldman et al. (1995)
   Assessments: Conduct problems

gg. Australian Twins (adults)
   Studies: Slutske, Heath et al. (1997)
   Assessments: Conduct problems

hh. Dutch Twins
   Studies: van den Oord et al. (1996)
   Assessments: Aggression

ii. Vietnam Era Twins
   Studies: Lyons et al. (1995), Coccaro et al. (1997)
   Assessments: Antisocial behaviors and aggression

jj. Nonshared Environment in Adolescent Development Twins
   Studies: Neiderhiser et al. (1998), O'Connor, McGuire et al. (1998), O'Connor, Neiderhiser et al. (1998), Deater-Deckard and Dodge (1997), Pike et al. (1996)
   Assessments: Antisocial behaviors

kk. Indian Twins
   Studies: Nathawat and Puri (1995)
   Assessments: Socialization, indirect aggression, and verbal aggression

ll. Swedish Twins (adults)
   Studies: Gustavsson et al. (1996)
   Assessments: Indirect aggression and verbal aggression

mm. Swedish Twins (children)
   Studies: Eley et al. (1999)
   Assessments: Aggression and delinquency

nn. British Twins
   Studies: Eley et al. (1999)
   Assessments: Aggression and Delinquency

oo. New York Twins
   Studies: Seelig and Brandon (1997)
   Assessments: Antisocial behavior

Classic Longitudinal Studies

Brunswick Study
   Sample Size/Population: 668 African-American males ages 12–17 years living in Harlem in 1967–1968 with follow-ups during ages 26–31 years
   Time: 1967–1981
   Assessments: Substance abuse.

Cairns Study
   Sample Size/Population: 695 boys and girls in 4th and 7th grades
   Time: 1981–1994
   Assessments: Children, parents, grandparents, and other caregivers were assessed with the focus being on aggression, school dropout, and gender differences.

Cohen and Brock Study
   Sample Size/Population: Random sample of 975 children, ages 1–10 years, living in upstate New York
   Time: 1975–1986
   Assessments: Psychiatric evaluations for each child and mother were conducted.

Douglas and Wadsworth Study
   Sample Size/Population: 5362 children from legitimate single births in England, Scotland, and Wales in 1 week of March 1946. Followed-up via criminal records to age 21 years
   Time: 1946–1967
   Assessments: Medical and school data were collected.

Elliott and Huizinga Study
   Sample Size/Population: U.S. representative sample of 1725 adolescents ages 11–17 years in 1976
      Time: 1976–1979
      Assessments: Arrest records were collected.

Eron and Huesmann Study
   Sample Size/Population: 875 8-year-old children in a semirural area of New York state
      Time: 1960–1982
      Assessments: Aggressive problem behavior was assessed.

Fergusson Study
   Sample Size/Population: 1265 children born in Christchurch, New Zealand in 1977
      Time: 1977-1992
      Assessments: Data were collected from mother, child, and teacher with a focus on self-reported delinquency and substance abuse.

S. Glueck and E. Glueck Study
   Sample Size/Population: 500 male delinquents in Massachusetts' correctional schools in 1939–1944 and 500 matched nondelinquents
      Time: 1939–1956
      Assessments: Antisocial and delinquent behavior.

Hawkins, Elliot, and Weiher Study
   Sample Size/Population: 1500 children (ages 7, 9, 11, 13, and 15 years) in high-risk neighborhoods in Denver, Colorado
      Time: 1988–present
      Assessments: High-risk behaviors and protective factors.

Janson and Wikström Study
   Sample Size/Population: 15,117 children born in Stockholm, Sweden in 1953 and living in Stockholm in 1963
      Time: 1963–1983
      Assessments: School testing, mothers were interviewed, and police records were analyzed.

Jessor Study

Sample Size/Population: 1126 high school student (grades 7–9) and 497 freshman college students

Time: 1969–1981

Assessments: Self-report measures of problem behaviors and substance abuse.

Kandel Study

Sample Size/Population: 8206 adolescents from a secondary school sample (grades 10–11) in New York State, as well as 5574 parents

Time: 1971–1990

Assessments: Substance abuse.

Kellam and Ensminger Study

Sample Size/Population: 1242 first graders in an African-American Chicago neighborhood (Woodlawn)

Time: 1966–1993

Assessments: Focused on shy and aggressive behaviors as well as substance abuse.

Le Blanc and Fréchette Study

Sample Size/Population: 3070 French-speaking Montreal, Quebec adolescents; 470 male delinquents at age 15, 17, and 22 years

Time: 1974–1987

Assessments: Antisocial conduct.

Loeber and Lahey Study

Sample Size/Population: 177 clinic-referred boys ages 7–12 years

Time: 1987–present

Assessments: Diagnostic assessments as well as other clinical measurements of behavior and functioning were conducted.

McCord and McCord Study

Sample Size/Population: 650 boys (average age 10 years) labeled difficult or average by Cambridge and Somerville, Massachusetts schools in 1937–1939

Time: 1937–1980

Assessments: Delinquent behaviors.

Miller and Kolvin Study
Sample Size/Population: All 1142 children born in Newcastle, England in May–June 1947
Time: 1947–1994
Assessments: Criminal activity and behaviors.

Patterson Study
Sample Size/Population: Follow-up of 206 4th grade boys in Eugene, Oregon first assessed in 1984
Time: 1984–1994
Assessments: Antisocial behaviors and parental behaviors.

Pulkkinen Study
Sample Size/Population: 369 children ages 8–9 years in Jyvaskyla, Finland in 1968
Time: 1968–1986
Assessments: Peer, teacher, and self-ratings were assessed.

Robins Study
Sample Size/Population: 524 children treated in a St. Louis, Missouri child guidance clinic in 1924–1929 and 100 public school children interviewed 30 years later; also 235 African-American males born in St. Louis in 1930–1934 and located in elementary school records
Time: 1924–1966
Assessments: Antisocial behaviors.

Rutter and Quinton Study
Sample Size/Population: All 1689 10-year-old children in an inner London, England borough attending state schools in 1970; and all 1279 10-year-old children on the Isle of Wright attending state schools in 1964
Time: 1970–1985
Assessments: Risk factors for childhood psychopathology.

Schwartzman Study
Sample Size/Population: All 324 French-Canadian first graders (age 7 years) in Montreal, Quebec
Time: 1978–1985

Assessments: Assessed by peers and self-reports, with a delinquency focus.

Silva and Moffit Study
Sample Size/Population: All 1037 children born in 1972–1973 in Dunedin, New Zealand (age 3 years)
Time: 1972–1987
Assessments: Biannual evaluations on health, psychological and antisocial behavior, and educational and family factors.

Thornberry, Lizotte, and Krohn Study
Sample Size/Population: All 1000 7th and 8th graders in 1988 disproportionally sampled from high crime neighborhoods
Time: 1988 to present
Assessments: Delinquency.

Tremblay Study
Sample Size/Population: All 1161 kindergarten boys in Montreal, Quebec
Time Variables: Early 1980s–present
Assessments: Children were assessed by teachers and followed up to age 12 years.

Verhulst Study
Sample Size/Population: All 2600 children ages 4–16 years from Zuid-Holland, first assessed in 1983
Time: 1983–1991
Assessments: Assessments of mental health functioning performed by mothers and self-reports.

Werner Study
Sample Size/Population: All 698 children from birth in Kauai, Hawaii, in 1955
Time: 1955–1987
Assessments: Health, education, and police records were collected.

West and Farrington Study

Sample Size/Population: All 411 boys ages 8–9 years in 1961–1962 in six London schools

Time: 1961–1994

Assessments: Delinquency.

White and Labouvie Study

Sample Size/Population: Stratified random sample of 1380 12, 15, and 18 year olds in New Jersey

Time: 1979–1987

Assessments: Substance abuse.

3

Administrative Data on Juveniles

INTRODUCTION

Administrative data offer unique opportunities for enhancing knowledge of the juvenile justice system and youth who are processed in it. The type and utility of administrative data sources vary across settings. This is because institutions and agencies involved in the juvenile justice system are all collecting information regarding characteristics of young people involved in the system. As such, decisions made about the care and control of these young people and the experiences and outcomes of these youth are affected. Consequently, administrative data sources offer opportunities to address a variety of questions pertaining to how young people are handled by this system and its various entities as well as to gain a broader understanding of the experiences and outcomes of youth in the juvenile justice system. Furthermore, the increasing ability and willingness to link data offers opportunities to examine the experiences of young people across both systems (e.g., juvenile justice, child welfare, and mental health) and time (e.g., childhood to adulthood).

This chapter facilitates research using administrative data by discussing the role and uses of these types of data in the juvenile justice system and providing techniques for building partnerships with and accessing administrative data from juvenile courts, detention centers, residential facilities, and community corrections offices. It offers innovative and practical approaches to managing the unique challenges and strategies associated with the use of administrative data, presents techniques for addressing related human subjects and ethical issues, and discusses issues related to the collection, management, and analysis of administrative data sources.

ROLE AND USES OF ADMINISTRATIVE DATA ON JUVENILES

Courts, institutions, and agencies in the juvenile justice system all collect information about young people involved in the system. This information is collected for a variety of purposes including establishing official records, reporting requirements of governmental or funding entities, identifying the characteristics, needs, and outcomes of young people involved in the system, tracking payments, and evaluating the effectiveness of programs and services. Administrative data often involve different types of information including arrests, petitions, adjudications, and dispositions, dates and types of offenses, outcomes of cases, characteristics of youth (e.g., race/ethnicity, gender, family structure, residence), involvement in other systems such as the child welfare system, evaluations conducted by probation officers or other service providers, assessments used to determine service needs, the types of programs in which a youth is involved, services received by a youth, and dates of program involvement. In many cases, courts or agencies will use the data to provide general reports or statistics and for internal uses such as managing dockets or caseloads. Some courts or agencies will use the data to examine program, decision making, or long-term outcomes.

Most courts and agencies, however, do not use the information they are collecting to its fullest potential. In large part, this is because these entities do not have the reason, expertise, or resources to do so. Consequently, there are opportunities for researchers to play this role and use administrative data to address a range of questions. Although the questions that may be addressed using administrative data sources vary considerably, for the purposes of this chapter two general categories of studies are identified. The first pertains to the "administration" of juvenile justice. Studies in this category typically focus on patterns of decision making in the juvenile justice system and provide knowledge on how juvenile courts and institutions dispose of cases and the factors that affect decisions at various points in the decision-making process. These types of studies are very important because they provide a picture of how the system is actually operating and spur debate over policy and practice. For example, administrative data have been used to explore the role of race and ethnicity in detention decisions (Shook & Goodkind, 2009; Rodriguez, 2007; Armstrong & Rodriguez, 2005; Bishop & Frazier, 1996; Wordes, Bynum, & Corley, 1994), decisions to treat juveniles as adults in the justice system (Shook, 2011; Sridharan, Greenfield, & Blakley, 2004; Podkopacz & Feld, 1996, 2001; Singer, 1993, 1996; Fagan & Deschenes, 1990; Fagan, Forst, & Vivona, 1987), the effects of defense counsel and geography in the juvenile court (Feld, 1991, 1993), and the role of child welfare involvement on juvenile court dispositions (Ryan, Herz, Hernandez, & Marshall, 2007).

A second category of studies involves those examining outcomes. These types of studies focus on assessing the impact of various experiences, decisions, or programs on outcomes such as recidivism. For example, numerous studies have compared the recidivism of youth transferred to the criminal court to those who were retained in the juvenile court (Myers, 2003; Fagan et al., 2003; Fagan, 1996; Bishop, Frazier, Lanza-Kaduce, & Winner, 1996). These studies have used administrative data to match youth or account for characteristics associated with offending and to track subsequent recidivism. Similarly, researchers have used administrative data to examine the movement of youth from the child welfare to the juvenile justice system in order to examine the relationship between specific youth characteristics and experiences and the likelihood of being involved in the juvenile justice system (Jonson-Reid, 2002; Jonson-Reid & Barth, 2000a, 2000b; Ryan, Herz, Hernandez, & Marshall, 2007). Researchers have also used administrative data to examine the effectiveness of specific programs or services in the juvenile justice system. Thus, there are numerous types of research questions that can be answered using administrative data. The next section of this chapter presents some of the advantages and limitations of using administrative data to address these questions.

ADVANTAGES AND LIMITATIONS OF ADMINISTRATIVE DATA IN JUVENILE JUSTICE

In addition to the range of different questions that can be answered, studies based on administrative data offer a number of other advantages to researchers studying the juvenile justice system. Administrative data are typically collected on each individual who comes through a particular institution or agency. What this means is that researchers often have access to samples that include the population of cases involved in that institution or agency, which provides the opportunity for researchers to gain access to large samples of youth. The availability of these types of samples increases the range of analyses that can be conducted and comparisons that can be made. Administrative data are often collected over time meaning that researchers have opportunities to analyze longitudinal data at much lower costs than studies based on survey or observational data collection methods. Because many courts and agencies have been collecting these data over time, administrative data also provide the opportunity to develop longitudinal designs based on existing data, thereby enabling results to be provided in a shorter time frame than longitudinal studies based on primary data collection. Furthermore, the increasing capacity and willingness to link data both within the juvenile justice system and across other systems add to the potential questions that may be asked and the types of studies that may be designed. Finally, for researchers interested in questions pertaining to the pattern and type of involvement of young people in the juvenile justice system, administrative data are often a more reliable source than retrospective reports about system experiences from youth themselves.

At the same time that administrative data offer many advantages, there can be numerous challenges and limitations associated with using these data for purposes of analysis. A major challenge is that administrative data are typically not collected in a manner designed to address research questions. In fact, most forms of administrative data in the juvenile justice system are designed for official record keeping purposes or to generate aggregate reports regarding case processing or decision making. Working with administrative data sources often involves extensive work to prepare the data files to get them ready for analysis, including having to work across a variety of files that contain data elements necessary to address the research question(s). Furthermore, although some administrative data sources are maintained electronically and can be transferred to statistical programs, other sources involve paper records or electronic records that cannot be transferred to statistical programs. Although these types of data sources present considerable challenges, they also offer opportunities to address important questions in the field and should be considered as a valuable source of data by researchers interested in the juvenile justice system.

Another challenge to working with administrative data is that there is often a lot of error associated with data entry. Data entry is typically the responsibility of clerks, interns, probation officers, or caseworkers, and there is often no check on its accuracy. Codes may also change over time, entire data fields will become obsolete, and courts and agencies might also change the way they enter or collect data and the systems they use for the collection of data. The interpretations researchers make regarding data fields might also differ from the meaning of those fields. For research questions that involve matching data across systems, there can be problems matching individuals and the likelihood of attrition because a family or individual has moved away from the jurisdiction covered by the court or agency. Finally, administrative data often lack the depth that can be gained from surveys, in-depth interviews, or ethnographic methods thereby limiting conclusions that can be drawn from these studies.

As such, it is important for researchers to thoroughly assess how administrative data help them answer their research question(s) and how such data fit into their broader research agenda. Although some research questions can be answered directly with administrative data, many questions require multiple forms of data collection. For example, administrative data can be useful for understanding patterns of case processing decisions in the juvenile court and factors associated with these decisions.

Yet, it is likely that factors not included in administrative data files also influence decision making, and researchers should incorporate other means of data collection in order to assess these factors and provide more context to the results generated from administrative data sources (for an example of this type of approach, see Shook, 2011). Furthermore, the lack of depth in many administrative data sources often requires researchers to collect other forms of data to provide more context and depth to findings. Thus, researchers interested in working with administrative data should fully conceptualize the role that administrative data will play in their work and seek to supplement it with other forms of data when necessary.

BUILDING PARTNERSHIPS AND GAINING ACCESS TO ADMINISTRATIVE DATA

Although there are many benefits to using administrative data to study the juvenile justice system, researchers must be aware that gaining access to administrative data requires time and relationship building. Juvenile courts and other agencies involved in the juvenile justice system are extremely busy places and the process of providing administrative data for research purposes requires substantial time and resources on behalf of the court or agency. Furthermore, the juvenile justice system, like other systems, is a highly political environment and courts and agencies might be apprehensive about getting involved in research because of the potential implications of negative or controversial findings. Courts, agencies, and institutions within the juvenile justice system might also be apprehensive about working with researchers because of past experiences in which researchers received data but did not provide the agency or institution with any tangible benefits or in which the results of a study were negative and perceived as harmful. In addition, the data necessary to answer some questions are likely to be located in different institutions or agencies (e.g., police, juvenile court, juvenile corrections) requiring researchers to work across settings to develop the data set necessary to complete the study.

Rarely, then, is acquiring administrative data as easy as having a court or agency just turn over its data to a researcher. Instead, researchers must be mindful that gaining access to administrative data requires them to build and maintain relationships with actors in these systems and that this takes time and patience. There is not one trick or method to building or maintaining these relationships. In some cases, court or agency administrators or directors are interested in developing relationships with researchers and may reach out to them or may be open to developing a relationship. In many other instances, administrators or directors need to be convinced of the utility of getting involved in the research process. Often, the key to gaining access to administrative data requires finding the right person, which may be difficult in many local and state juvenile justice systems in which there are multiple agencies and actors.

To build relationships within the juvenile justice system, it is often easier to use contacts or networks then cold calling. It is likely that someone within your school or department has contacts with local or state agencies of interest and the use of contacts can help identify the right person to talk to and facilitate meetings. If not, it can be helpful to use contacts within the community who might have relationships with actors in the system. Regardless of the process through which contacts are made, it is necessary for the researcher to do his or her "homework" before approaching a court, institution, or agency. This requires learning all that you can about the organization, what it does, who the key players are, and what type of information it collects. It is also important to gain an understanding of the "politics" of the environment and to get a sense of who the key players are in that environment and where conflicts might exist. This process will take some time and it is likely that you will not have access to a lot of information about the broader environment at the start of the process. It is important, however, to gain as much information as possible and to consciously seek to increase your understanding about the local or state environment as you proceed to set up meetings, gain access to data, and produce and report the results of the study.

Gaining a sense of the environment is especially important for projects that require collecting information across courts and institutions, as is common for many studies in the juvenile justice system. The juvenile justice system, like its criminal justice counterpart, consists of a variety of "loosely coupled" actors, institutions, and agencies. Youth often move from one agency or institution to the next and each collects data pertaining to its function or information-collecting requirements. Even within one setting, such as a court, data may be collected within different departments (e.g., intake, clerk's office, probation) and never formally linked together. Therefore, a researcher seeking to link data across decision-making points must work to develop and build relationships across and within these settings.

Regardless of whether you are working within one setting or across multiple settings, it is important to identify one or two people who will serve as "sponsors" for a project. A sponsor is someone who is interested in and supportive of your idea and can provide you with the necessary legitimacy and contacts. The sponsor does not need to be the person at the top of an organization's hierarchy. It is helpful, however, if this person has contacts and legitimacy within the system, understands the value of research, and has some authority within the system. The role of the sponsor is to help you gain access to data within a particular setting and to help you establish the contacts and legitimacy necessary to gain access to data from other institutions or actors in the system.

It is also necessary to realize the distinction between those who have the authority to provide data and those who actually do most of the work to provide the data. Although not always the case, those with the authority to provide the data often do not do the actual work necessary to provide the data to you. This can create a tension and lead to potential problems, as in many cases those who are responsible for doing the work already have significant responsibilities and you want to avoid being viewed, as much as possible, as just another item on their plate. Furthermore, sometimes those who have authority to provide you with the data do not always know what is in the data or how long it might take to extract the data. Developing relationships with those who know the data is also important because these are the individuals who are most likely to understand the strengths, limitations, and meanings of particular data fields. Thus, the researcher should try to be as aware as possible of the dynamics involved, to develop a relationship with those who know the data, and to be patient and respectful in the process. If the project is part of a grant proposal, the researcher should consider writing at least part of the agency's time into the budget if permitted.

In seeking to develop relationships within the juvenile justice system for the purpose of gaining access to administrative data, it is important to have a clear conceptualization of the study you would like to conduct. At the same time, it is equally, if not more, important to be flexible in your research design and to understand what is necessary to conduct the study you want and how willing you are to change the study design as the process unfolds. Conducting research in the juvenile justice system is difficult and preferred research designs are not always possible in the field, including studies involving administrative data. It is clearly necessary to pursue rigorous research designs, but researchers must be flexible enough and willing to adapt their design to fit what is possible and to adapt to changing circumstances when necessary.

It is also necessary, when developing and building relationships, to give something back to the actors and agencies involved in the study. As noted previously, it takes time and resources to provide access to data, and courts, agencies, and institutions in the juvenile justice system are often very busy and lack resources. Researchers seeking to work with administrative data, then, should recognize this and be willing to provide something such as a report and/or presentation for the court or agency. In fact, one way to develop relationships is to volunteer to do research for a court or agency on a question that is important or of interest to them. By doing so, one can build the necessary relationships and gain legitimacy in the system.

In sum, gaining access to administrative data is time consuming and requires developing and building relationships. One suggestion is to conceptualize the process as a collaborative relationship. Although many individuals within the juvenile justice system are interested in learning more about what they are doing and what effects it is having, everyone involved in the research also has an interest in the process. Finding ways to work together to increase knowledge and serve these interests can help develop a long-term relationship that opens the door for additional projects that build upon or expand existing work. Doing so can be especially fruitful given the time it takes to develop and maintain these relationships and opportunities.

HUMAN SUBJECTS AND ETHICAL ISSUES

Unlike studies featuring primary data collection, research projects using administrative data have the advantage of being easier to get approved by the Institutional Review Board (IRB). Children and prisoners both receive considerable protections in the research process. Data collection involving children who are prisoners is very difficult to get approved by the IRB and researchers are often limited in what they are able to do in these settings. Although the reasons for these protections and the stringency of the process are good, the IRB process can still be extremely frustrating for researchers seeking to collect data from young people in the juvenile justice system. Because studies using administrative data do not involve collecting data directly from the individual child, it is often possible that these studies can be defined as exempt by the IRB if they meet certain criteria. Below, we briefly discuss strategies for gaining approval to conduct studies using administrative data from the juvenile justice system.

Similar to studies involving primary data collection, the most important thing for a researcher is to meet with a staff member at the IRB and talk about the study. The staff at the IRB often has substantial experience with various study designs and can provide the input necessary to structure the study and protocol in a way that gains IRB approval. In the case of studies using administrative data, this discussion can often determine whether the study could be determined to be "exempt." Exempt studies are those that are based on preexisting data, documents, or records (those that are currently in existence) and do not contain any personally identifying information. This means that if an agency is willing to provide its data without identifiable information, the study is exempt from IRB review. Many studies using administrative data fall within this category, and researchers are often able to gain approval fairly quickly. In instances in which the study involves linking data across court, institutions, or agencies, exempt status is still possible even though there is a need to provide a common identifier. This is often achieved through the use of an "honest broker," someone who serves as an intermediary between the researcher and individuals being studied. The honest broker must be someone who is not involved in the research and has legitimate access to the data.

In addition to the IRB at your academic institution, sometimes local or state agencies will have an IRB process as well. This is particularly common when working with the Department of Corrections, but is required at times when conducting research in the juvenile justice system or with specific agencies. Researchers should look into whether these requirements exist prior to starting the project so that they can plan their time accordingly. In situations in which the data contain identifying information, the study cannot be defined as exempt and the researcher must go through the typical IRB review process. This can become complicated and we refer you to the discussion in Chapters 1 and 4 to learn more about how to navigate the IRB to conduct research in the justice systems. Again, we highly recommend working with your institutional IRB to plan your study and determine what you need to do to comply with human subjects protections.

DATA COLLECTION, MANAGEMENT, AND ANALYSIS

One of the advantages of many projects that use administrative data is that the researcher or research team often does not need to be on "site" collecting the data. Although not true of some projects, administrative data can often be provided via a data management or statistical program from the court or agency. This can save a tremendous amount of time and the type of delivery can be worked out with the research or information management staff at the court or agency. Sometimes courts or agencies will have "codebooks" that provide a list and description of available variables. Often, however, a codebook is not available and researchers must use screen shots or other sources of information to determine which variables they would like to acquire. It is helpful for the researcher to be clear in what he or she would like in discussions with research staff or the information management people at the court or agency. The researcher should, though, understand that being too specific can run the risk of neglecting various data elements that might be useful to the study. One suggestion, then, is to start with a list of various domains and work with the court or agency to identify the data elements that are available and fit within those domains. Asking for as much as possible is preferable in some respects because it limits the possibility that information is being missed. At the same time, researchers must be careful about what they ask for in the data request and should try to find out as much as possible about what is available prior to the final request.

As noted previously, it is also likely that the data are not in a form that lends itself to analysis and it is likely that the data will require a substantial amount of preparation for analysis. For example, data about a single individual may be provided on multiple lines representing different events or contacts. This requires the researcher to make decisions regarding how the dataset and specific variables should be constructed. Similarly, it is likely that the data will be provided in multiple files requiring that they be linked through a common identifier. Although this is clearly manageable, it opens up the possibility of error or problems in the matching process and researchers need to be very careful in the process. Given the complexity involved in some projects using administrative data, it is important that researchers ensure that they have access to individuals who have expertise in working with these types of data sets. When conceptualizing grant applications, it is advisable to include room in the budget for individuals who have the expertise and experience necessary to help get the files ready for analysis.

Another key to working with administrative data sets is that the researcher needs to communicate with the court or agency to determine what specific data fields or codes actually represent. As mentioned previously, sometimes specific codes will stop being used or might mean something different than they appear to mean. Consequently, it is important for researchers to work with individuals at the court or agency to understand how information is entered, what various data elements include, what codes mean, and what kinds of error are commonly associated with data entry. This requires continual communication and researchers should always check with agencies prior to reporting on a particular variable.

ADDITIONAL RESOURCES

The focus of this chapter was on the valuable role that administrative data can play in research on the juvenile justice system and techniques and tips on how to gain access to and work with administrative data. Yet, not all administrative data need to be obtained from courts or agencies in the juvenile justice system. The Office of Juvenile Justice and Delinquency Prevention (OJJDP) routinely collects information from courts and agencies that can be used in the research process. The potential uses of this information in the research process vary, but it offers another source of information that researchers can use. Similarly, the National Center for Juvenile Justice (NCJJ) collects data from court systems that are available for researchers to use. Researchers interested in learning more about these data sources should visit the websites of OJJDP (www.ojjdp.gov) and NCJJ (www.ncjj.org). Other entities at the state or local level might also have administrative data sources available, and researchers should seek to learn more about these sources as well.

ADDITIONAL READING

Schwartz, R. M., Gagnon, D. E., Muri, J. H., Zhao, Q. R., & Kellogg, R. (1999). Administrative data for quality improvement. *Pediatrics, 103* (1 Suppl E), 291–301.

This article describes the valuable use of administrative data for quality improvement in perinatal and neonatal medical settings. Many of the principles are applicable to juvenile justice systems as well.

4

Field Research with Adults in the Criminal Justice System

INTRODUCTION

We use the term "criminal justice system" to refer to a vast array of entities that work with individuals who have been accused or convicted of violating the law. The titles placed on people involved in the criminal justice system are also varied depending on which criminal justice agency individuals encounter. These individuals are referred to as defendants, probationers, inmates, prisoners, parolees, offenders, and other terms. Because there are many different criminal justice entities mentioned in this chapter, we refer to all individuals involved in the criminal justice system as "clients." We define the criminal justice system as including drug court, mental health court, probation, jail, prison, and parole/postrelease supervision.[1] Throughout the chapter examples of these different sectors of the criminal justice system are described.[2] We use the following working definitions:

- *Drug court*: Courts designed and designated to handle cases involving clients with psychoactive substance use disorders. The general goal of drug courts is to reduce the incidence of reoffending and promote rehabilitation from substance abuse through intensive judicial supervision and referral to services (National Criminal Justice Reference Service, 2011).

- *Mental health court*: Specialized courts that refer clients to mental health treatment and services in lieu of incarceration. Mental health court clients are generally supervised by a team composed of the court judge, court-related personnel, and community treatment providers partnering with the court. Successful completion of the mandated treatment plan usually results in resolution of the case.
- *Probation*: Supervision in the community of adults who have been convicted of an offense. Clients often serve their entire sentence in the community, although some jurisdictions have split sentences in which the client is incarcerated for a period of the sentence and then is supervised in the community for a period of the sentence. In many instances, a client's failure to abide by the terms of probation will result in incarceration.
- *Jail*: Jails are typically owned and operated by a county or regional government. They house clients accused of offenses, awaiting trial, awaiting transfer to another facility after conviction, as well as clients convicted of minor offenses (usually with a sentence of less than 1 year). In some cases, the state government will contract with jails to house state prisoners because of lack of space in the prisons.
- *Prison*: Prisons are owned by states or the federal government. They typically hold people convicted of felony offenses with sentences of more than a year, but this varies by state. Private prisons are those run by a private cooperation that has contracted with the state or federal government to house prisoners. Six states combine jails and prisons.
- *Parole/postrelease supervision*: This refers to the conditional release of a client from prison to serve the remainder of a sentence in the community. Historically, people on parole were released to parole by a parole board decision. Currently, many states have replaced parole board releases with mandatory release/ parole as a provision of statute. This means, for instance, that

after a person serves 85% of the sentence in prison, statute requires that the person serve the remaining 15% of the sentence in the community. Some states continue to refer to this status as parole, whereas others refer to this status as postrelease supervision. In many jurisdictions a violation of the conditional release conditions of parole results in a return to incarceration.

COMMON RESEARCH DESIGNS IN CRIMINAL JUSTICE RESEARCH

Over the past decade, criminologically focused researchers have pushed for the use of more rigorous research designs and statistical methods. Most notably, there is a dearth of experimental evaluations in field research in criminal justice settings. Although in recent years more experimental research has been conducted, experimental designs make up only 4% of research designs in top criminal justice journals (Kleck, Tark, & Bellows, 2006). The most common designs used are cross-sectional (60%) and longitudinal (26%) research approaches. Data are primarily gathered using survey methods (45%) and archival data (32%). The most common statistical methods are linear and logistic regression models with less than 7% of research articles using more complex statistical methods (Kleck, Tark, & Bellows, 2006). Intervention research and evaluation research conducted by criminologists have been criticized as lacking in theoretical frameworks, fidelity assessments, and dosage evaluations (Taxman & Friedman, 2009). The current state of criminological research demonstrates the enormous opportunity for social work field researchers to add to the extant literature.

ACCESS: DEVELOPING PARTNERSHIPS

Partnering with criminal justice agencies is much different than partnering with other types of community agencies. Unlike some community partnerships in which the agency contacts a university to conduct evaluations, in criminal justice settings a university researcher will more often contact criminal justice agencies to inquire about a research project. When thinking about partnering with a criminal justice agency, it is important to remember that the criminal justice system is vast and interconnected. The job duties of people working at any given level of the criminal justice system are often dictated by legislation and the activities of other entities in the criminal justice system. For example, courts do not have authority over who walks into their courtroom (i.e., who becomes clients of the court). Courtroom clients are people the police have arrested and accused of a given offense. Similarly, the prison system does not determine who is imprisoned in their institutions. Prisons receive those people who have been convicted by the court system. The prison system also has little control over when people leave prison. Sentences are determined by courts, and the range of sentences that can be applied is often determined by legislators. Legislators' sentencing guidelines are heavily influenced by the political climate of that year and locale. Given the number of factors that control everyday decision making of any given agency within the criminal justice system, it logically follows that although potentially welcome, engaging in university research partnerships may be viewed as yet another "outside" entity that has the potential to complicate daily agency functioning. Successful researchers will honor this "outsider" status when attempting to develop partnerships.

Criminal justice entities are bombarded with inquires from researchers, the public, and the media. Researchers wanting to conduct studies within criminal justice agencies should adhere to three key principles:

1. View establishing and maintaining relationships as the primary goal and the research agenda as a secondary goal.
2. Ensure the research project is mutually beneficial.
3. Be flexible and patient.

Establishing and maintaining relationships with criminal justice agencies require that the researcher recognize that the primary role of criminal justice agencies is to maintain public safety. This is the case despite the approach criminal justice agencies take toward achieving that goal—retribution, deterrence, or rehabilitation. Although research is certainly valued in many criminal justice venues, it is unlikely that research projects will be on an agency's priority list. However, when researchers have established and worked to maintain a positive working relationship with these community partners, their research projects are more likely to be received and viewed favorably. Furthermore, as problems arise in the research project, as they almost certainly will, a strong collaborative relationship will help the researcher to maintain the best possible integrity of the study. In essence, researchers must first be willing to do the relationship work needed to pursue longer term research goals and funding collaboratively.

Successful research partnerships with criminal justice agencies are mutually beneficial. Examples of research projects that are *not* mutually beneficial and may not be well received by criminal justice entities fall into one of two categories: researchers who say their project will help "fix" the criminal justice system or researchers who say their research will "expose" major flaws in the criminal justice system. Although these project goals are certainly valid and important, they do little to address how the research is helpful to the criminal justice agency hosting the research project. Leaving aside for the moment the potential political and legal hotbed an agency may be left in with such research approaches, it is important to recognize that the time criminal justice partners spend on collaborative research projects is often donated time. If the proposed research question makes an agency defensive, requires unreimbursed time from agency staff, and offers little or no benefit to the agency in return, what incentive does an agency have to work with the researcher? Given the proper concern and consideration, it is not difficult to establish a research project that is mutually beneficial while also investigating critical topics. Questions to ask criminal justice agencies in order to establish such a project include the following:

- If you had all of the resources needed to find out about XYZ, what questions would you want answered?
- What information do you need to help you provide XYZ services to the extent that you would like to?

- We recognize that analyzing data about XYZ mostly benefits our research needs; are there additional data we could collect or analyze that would answer key questions for your agency?

Research within criminal justice field settings does not happen quickly. Working to develop and maintain partnerships and working to identify mutually beneficial research projects are timely endeavors. Like many field research sites, it is also likely that researchers will be working with people at multiple administrative layers. For example, in jails, the Sheriff may approve the research project, but the people who will facilitate data collection are administrators at the jail who will delegate responsibilities to program staff and correctional officers. Working out logistical issues and developing rapport with people at each level take time and patience. Additionally, higher level administrators might not understand some of the logistical requirements that make certain aspects of the research design not feasible. In those cases researchers will need to be flexible enough to work within the logistical constraints of the research site and make changes to certain aspects of the research protocol as needed. In these circumstances, explaining to the "data collection gate-keepers" (such as correctional officers) why you want to gather information in a certain way and asking for ideas about how to achieve this goal in a way that is logistically feasible often constitute a successful approach to meeting your project goals. Additionally, this type of flexibility honors the line-staff professionals' time, concerns, and expertise.

ASSESSMENT

Unfortunately for social work researchers, a dearth of psychosocial instruments exists for criminal justice populations. This is particularly the case for incarcerated samples. Therefore, field researchers must be creative about efficient means for collecting data. Fortunately, criminal justice agencies often use risk assessment instruments that have been developed specifically for criminal justice populations or otherwise are mandated to collect copious amounts of information on clients.

Risk assessments and administrative data are excellent resources for field researchers who want to collect a lot of information while also not taxing the agency or the study participants' time.

Administrative data are discussed elsewhere in this book, but field researchers can also take advantage of such data. Many researchers make the mistake of asking criminal justice entities what variables/data the agency collects. These researchers likely intend to look through the data and decide which variables are relevant to a given research project. Generally, asking criminal justice agencies what data they collect is an ineffective approach to getting research needs met. Instead, field researchers should spend time in advance thinking through their research questions and the types of data that will best answer those questions. At that point, the researcher can go to the criminal justice agency and ask questions such as: How do you know if a drug court client has a mental illness? How do you determine in what custody level an inmate should be housed? Do you record this information in an information management system? How is information about clients communicated between prosecutors and judges or institutional case managers and parole boards?

Assessment tools used by criminal justice agencies, often called "risk assessments," also contain information in which field researchers may be interested. Courts use presentencing investigation reports, drug courts assess severity of substance use and potential responsiveness to treatment, and a number of risk assessment tools have been developed for community corrections agencies and prisons to determine supervision stipulations for their clients. Examples of risk assessments include Level of Service Inventory-Revised (LSI-R), Psychopathy Checklist Revised (PCL-R), Historical, Clinical, and Risk Management Risk Assessment-20 (HCR-20), and Custody Ratings Scale (CRS). Recent meta-analysis articles also compare and contrast risk assessments (Campbell, French, & Gendreau, 2009; Hanson & Morton-Bourgon, 2009; Walters, 2006).

Few centralized databases of psychosocial assessments normed for criminal justice populations exist. Texas Christian University has developed a set of psychosocial assessments normed on criminal justice populations (http://www.ibr.tcu.edu/pubs/datacoll/listofforms.html). The University of Washington also has a database of substance abuse assessment instruments and descriptions of these instruments indicate when the instrument has been normed on a criminal justice population (http://adai.washington.edu/). Field researchers can also contribute to the literature by assessing the reliability of standardized instruments they chose to use in their own research projects (see Chapter 6).

IMPORTANCE OF THINKING ABOUT THE FUTURE

Conducting research in criminal justice settings in an efficient manner requires extensive future planning. Researchers must anticipate the lengthy approval process from universities and criminal justice agencies, the high mobility of people in and out of the criminal justice system, and the interconnectedness of criminal justice agencies and clients. Human subjects approval from universities is discussed later in this chapter. It is not uncommon for criminal justice agencies to also have their own internal review board for research applications. In those instances, the agency should be able to give researchers an approximate review and approval time as well as notify researchers if there is an expectation that researchers have secured approval from their university prior to submitting an application to the agency review board. Although researchers are accustomed to the time involved with university review boards, if the researchers have not planned ahead, they may not anticipate the review time also required by the criminal justice agency.

Another easily underestimated area of criminal justice research is the high mobility of clients in and out of any given criminal justice agency. Field researchers can plan for client mobility by working with criminal justice partners in advance to understand the average length of time clients are involved in the agency and the frequency with which a client will cease involvement with the agency and then return to the agency at a later date. For example, probation clients may abscond from probation temporarily. Abscond means the client stopped showing up for appointments with the probation officer, but this same client may return for appointments again at a later date. Alternatively, a probation client may have had his or her probation status revoked and thus was required to serve a jail or prison sentence for a number of months. But the client will be back on probation once that sentence is served. Understanding client mobility will help researchers to determine the study window, the nature of data to be collected and from whom, as well as ways to account or plan for attrition.

As with any research project, studies within the criminal justice system will lead to new research questions. Because of the complexity of the criminal justice system, these new questions may entail a need for researchers to collaborate with other criminal justice agencies. For example, if researchers are interested in continuity of healthcare treatment for people releasing from prisons, the researcher will need to understand what type of care prisoners/former prisoners received in the jail in which they were housed as well as the prison from which they were released. In many states, convicted offenders have spent a portion of their sentence in a jail prior to coming to the prison. Sometimes this is while the client is awaiting sentencing after conviction, but other times it is because the prison may not have space for that client yet and has contracted with the jail to house the client until prison space has opened. Because research questions may necessitate crossing multiple boundaries, researchers interactions with the first criminal justice agency are best regarded as just one in a series of interactions that the researcher will have in the future with other criminal justice agencies.

RACE AND ETHNICITY

The disproportionate representation of racial and ethnic minority groups in the criminal justice system makes careful attention to diversity critical to conducting representative field research. Field researchers will need to work with criminal justice partners to understand the demographic of the client population. In almost any criminal justice setting, researchers should consider stratified sampling approaches to obtain a representative sample. Moreover, researchers must keep in mind that in addition to the dearth of research instruments normed on criminal justice populations, there is equally an abundance of instruments that have been normed on largely white samples that possibly limit the reliability and validity of assessment instruments for other racial and ethnic minority groups. Using multiple measures to assess the same construct will help address this issue. Incorporating qualitative measures into studies will also help researchers to assess the nuances of measures and additional data that may need to be collected to better represent a largely nonwhite sample.

Language barriers are becoming an increasingly important factor in field research. Although many languages are spoken among criminal justice populations, Latinos are overrepresented in the criminal justice system—particularly in prisons. Relatedly, researchers must take great care to understand the implications of research participation for immigration status. Prison researchers will also run into deportation and Immigration and Naturalization Services (INS) complications.

IMPLEMENTATION

Timing, establishing buy-in, and understanding organizational culture are primary implementation factors that will influence a field researcher's success. As discussed in earlier sections, timing the implementation of the study will largely be influenced by timing requirements of both the university and the criminal justice setting Institutional Review Boards. Moreover, some criminal justice agencies will have a formal "research request" process in place. Field researchers should start the research approval processes at a minimum of 6 months in advance. Other more subtle timing issues are also ever-present when conducting research within the criminal justice settings. Keeping in mind that the criminal justice system is largely controlled by state legislators or county commissioners, there are certain times when research start-up will be more ideal than others. For example, trying to start up a research project with a state Department of Corrections immediately before or during a state legislative session can be problematic and lead to significant delays. During the relationship building process getting an understanding of when the heaviest external time demands are placed on the entity in question will not only demonstrate the researcher's consideration of the agency's constraints, but also make it more likely that the research project will be given the best chance of a timely start up. Keep in mind that the times of the year that are best for the criminal justice agencies may be in direct conflict with the times of the year that are best for university calendars. Accommodating the community partner's schedule is a sacrifice that field researchers often have to make.

Making sure to have met with and established a general agreement about the research protocols with the key gatekeepers in advance is critical to study implementation. As discussed earlier, criminal justice entities are often rigid hierarchical management structures and researchers will need project buy-in from top administrators as well as line staff. It is good practice to meet with all parties individually well in advance. During these meetings, especially with line staff that may have less background on what the researchers are trying to do, researchers want to accomplish three goals: (1) provide an overview of the project and emphasize why the researcher thinks this is important, (2) ask for feedback or thoughts about the project, and (3) ask about concerns that should be addressed in advance in order to agree upon a study protocol. These meetings also provide a good opportunity to ask questions about organizational culture.

Keeping in mind that safety and security are generally the top priority in criminal justice agencies, it is important to understand how the organization maintains safety and security in their daily operations. In essence, what is the organizational culture around interactions with that organization's clients, and specifically around safety and security issues? The primary considerations are security clearance, dress code, and the types of materials outsiders (e.g., research team members) are allowed to bring with them to the project site. When conducting research in state prisons, it is common for the prison system to require that a background check is performed for security clearance, that research team members should dress conservatively (e.g., sleeved shirts, nice pants or long skirts, closed toed shoes), and that research team members should bring a driver's license and only pen/pencil and paper into an agency (e.g., rarely are cell phones, audio/video recorders, and other electronic devices allowed in these settings). It is also wise for researchers to understand the acronyms and jargon specific to the agency of interest. Although some criminal justice language is universal, other references vary by region.

Other important organizational culture issues include the expectations of staff interactions with clients. For example, in a clinical setting for people with substance addictions, therapists will likely hold therapeutic alliance of primary importance. In a drug court, the drug court judge, attorneys, and case management staff are more likely to first consider public safety, then assess manipulation or lying on the part of the client, and third consider therapeutic factors. These issues are important to keep in mind when assessing the potential role of different agency professionals in the study—even roles as limited as being the first contact with the client about the research project. In general, a clear understanding of and respect for the organizational culture will communicate the researcher's awareness and consideration of the daily struggles the criminal justice professionals confront. This approach also helps to develop and maintain a good rapport with the community partner, which is particularly important when challenges arise for the current and future studies.

HUMAN SUBJECTS IN CRIMINAL JUSTICE RESEARCH

Field researchers can generally assume that the University Human Subjects Board has reviewed projects involving criminal justice populations. However, it is less likely that these same board members frequently see applications including criminal justice populations for behavioral science research. Given this, consider the human subjects application as an educational opportunity for the reviewers in addition to an instrument used to receive approval for a research project. Because most criminal justice populations are considered "protected populations" and because the University Review Board is likely to have less familiarity with criminal justice populations, make sure to submit human subjects applications as early as possible. This will give the field research team ample opportunity to address review board concerns ahead of time.

Additionally, because of the possibility that some of the information collected from individuals may be incriminating, the board may require a federal *Certificate of Confidentiality*. This certificate provides additional protections to the research participant. National Institutes of Health provides detailed information on these certificates at http://grants.nih.gov/grants/policy/coc/.

The following section will outline three strategies for facilitating a successful review.

Strategy 1: Be familiar with other studies that have done similar research and try to discern from the articles or by contacting the researchers directly what steps were taken to protect human subjects. Being able to cite this research will show the review board that other studies have used similar approaches and increase the credibility of the proposal.

Strategy 2: Contact the review board director or other representative as frequently as possible before submitting the application. Ask the contact for feedback on proposed research protocols in advance and for suggestions for revising these protocols. These strategies will likely reduce the number of revisions and reviews and may also help the researcher to think of other issues that may arise when the board is reviewing the application. Furthermore, the Chair will have a sense of what specific factors may cause the greatest concern or hesitation among other review board members. Often, universities include a community-based (i.e., external) criminal justice representative on the review board. Ask the Review Board Chair if the criminal justice representative may be contacted in advance so that the research team can similarly become aware of and address any issues the representative may foresee.

Strategy 3: Before submitting the application the researcher should fully address the following questions: (1) How is the safety and privacy of the participants maintained? (2) How is the safety of the research team maintained? (3) What are all of the ways in which the benefits of the research project to society, to the agency, and to the individual participants outweigh the risks posed to participants; and (4) Keeping in mind that risks of coercion are much greater in criminal justice settings, throughout the application the researcher should acknowledge the risks for coercion and detail how the research team will determine if coercion has occurred or is likely to occur. Then clearly list the specific steps the research team will take to prevent coercion.

Researchers may avoid studies with criminal justice populations because of horror stories they have heard about obtaining approval from Human Subjects Review Boards. Although this type of research presents more challenges than some other studies, it is possible to conduct high-quality research that is fully supported by the Board. Following the strategies outlined above will ease this process for field researchers.

BUILDING AND TRAINING A RESEARCH TEAM

Criminal justice-involved populations are shadowed by stigma. When building a research team, there has to be a realistic acknowledgment that people who have committed (or are accused of committing) criminal offenses are intimidating or "scary" to some people. Moreover, the media and other social misnomers may have influenced people's perceptions about who becomes and remains involved with the criminal justice system. Building a research team requires that education about the characteristics of criminal justice populations be provided to team members in advance. This training component should also include frank conversations about research team members' perceptions of criminal justice-involved individuals.

Alternatively, research team members' perceptions of the criminal justice-involved individuals may not be problematic, but rather the research team member's perception of the criminal justice system could interfere with objectivity. Some research team members may believe that the criminal justice system is severely corrupt and needs to be "fixed." They may believe that criminal justice professionals do not have the best interest of the client group in mind or do not actively exercise the best interest of the client group. Regardless of what perceptions research team members may have, it is important that their biases, myths, and thoughts about the criminal justice system are assessed and addressed.

Finally, when conducting research with criminal justice populations field researchers are likely to encounter research participants who have impairments in multiple areas: mental health, addictions, infectious diseases, risks of suicide, threats of violence, or criminal offenses for which the participant has not been convicted. Regardless of whether research instruments ask about any of these issues, they are still likely to surface. Protocols on how to handle disclosure (or attempt to prevent disclosure) should be established well in advance. Research team members should be trained on these protocols initially as well as revisiting case scenarios throughout the project.

DISSEMINATION

There is hardly an area of social work research that does not overlap with criminal justice-involved populations including: health, mental health, addictions, disenfranchisement, housing, veterans, child welfare, and aging. Because of this, the outlets for dissemination of research are as infinite as the research topics. Increasing numbers of abstracts on criminal justice-based research are being accepted at major social work conferences such as the *Council on Social Work Education* and *Society of Social Work and Research* annual program meetings. Research with criminal justice populations is also presented at the annual meetings of the *American Public Health Association* and the *American Society of Criminology, Academy of Criminal Justice Sciences, and American Psychology-Law Society*. International organizations such as the *International Association of Forensic Mental Health Services* and the *International Academy of Law and Mental Health* also feature social work research at annual conferences. Like any research topic, social work research should be matched with the journal. Criminal justice journals with high impact factors (see Chapter 6 for a discussion on impact factors) include the following: *Criminology, Journal of Research on Crime & Delinquency, Criminal Justice and Behavior, Sexual Abuse: A Journal of Research and Treatment,* and *Journal of Interpersonal Violence.* According to a survey of the Academy of Criminal Justice Sciences members (Kleck, Tark, & Bellows, 2006), the seven leading criminal justice journals are *Criminology, Journal of Criminal Law and Criminology, Justice Quarterly, Journal of Research in Crime and Delinquency, Crime and Delinquency, Journal of Criminal Justice,* and *Journal of Quantitative Criminology.* Intervention and evaluation research is commonly published in journals such as *Criminal Justice and Behavior* and the *Journal of Experimental Criminology.* In addition to academic outlets for research, social workers are well-positioned to disseminate research findings to agency administrators and policy-makers with the goal of influencing social and program policy decisions.

CASE EXAMPLE[3]

Support Matters is a social support intervention for recently released prisoners with substance use disorders. Manualized to ensure fidelity, *Support Matters* uses a cognitive-behavioral approach to promote involvement in positive social support networks that will, in turn, promote commitment to positive social norms and the incorporation of cognitions that will reduce the impact of risk factors for continued substance misuse and criminal behavior. Prior to release from prison, participants identify a known positive support partner in the community. After release, the prisoner–partner dyads attend 10 weekly group sessions of skills and cognitive-behavioral training. The program aims to reconfigure a person's social network from one dominated by antisocial behaviors (e.g., people who misuse psychoactive substances and engage in criminal behaviors) to a social network supportive of the person's desistance from substance misuse and crime. Meeting with up to four other dyads, the support partners and the former prisoner participants work together to establish realistic expectations, develop reciprocity of support, and learn the skills necessary to implement strategies to reduce the likelihood of participants' relapse to substance misuse or criminal behaviors.

Support Matters was recently pilot tested in North Carolina using a randomized controlled trial (RCT) design. *Support Matters* was tested at an established community agency that has been serving former prisoners for 20 years. The study used a two-group, treatment and control group design with a third comparison group condition. Primary observations included standardized measures that were delivered to *treatment* and *control* participants at four time points—prerelease, preintervention, postintervention, and a 3-month follow-up after the intervention. To reduce attrition, weekly measures were also collected for *treatment* and *control* conditions during the first 12 weeks postrelease and then every 3 weeks for the last 12 weeks of the postrelease data collection period. *Comparison group* participant data included prerelease interviews and postrelease administrative data.

DEVELOPING PARTNERSHIPS FOR *SUPPORT MATTERS*

The *Support Matters* trial required community partnerships with the North Carolina Department of Correction (DOC) that oversees both community corrections (probation and parole) and all of the state prisons, 10 individual state prisons, and a community-based service delivery agency. Because RCT projects can be met with resistance and because the pilot trial was lengthy and quite extensive ($N = 197$), the principal investigator (PI) first conducted a much smaller preliminary study. The preliminary study allowed the PI to collect important data for the trial, but even more critical, it allowed the PI to understand some of the dynamics of the DOC, the prisons, and the community in which the *Support Matters* trial was ultimately to be delivered. Moreover, it gave the community partners a chance to get to know the PI and to give the PI feedback about the types of information that would be helpful for the DOC.

The PI spent approximately 1 year meeting with DOC partners and conducting the preliminary study. During this year, it became clear that it would be more beneficial to the DOC for the PI to conduct her research in a county that was 2 hours away from her university office. The PI ultimately conducted the preliminary study and the *Support Matters* trial in that county as a way to make the project mutually beneficial to her research agenda and the DOC. Also during that year, the PI was able to better understand the needs and culture of the DOC, identify gaps in information collected by the DOC, identify a community partner to deliver the intervention, identify prison-based recruitment sites, and get to know the administrative data that were available to supplement data collection for the *Support Matters* trial. Once the DOC central administrative office approved of the project, the PI set up individual meetings with each of the 10 prison-based recruitment sites to address any questions or concerns the prisons may have had and to establish agreed upon research protocols.

DATA AND MEASUREMENT

The *Support Matters* trial included data collection prior to a participant's release from prison and for approximately 6 months after a participant's release from prison. Data collection tools included standardized instruments, qualitative interviews, surveys designed specifically for the project, and administrative data. Because of difficulties in finding measures that have been normed on a criminal justice population, the PI used multiple measures of each construct. For example, substance misuse was measured pre- and postrelease with a total of six standardized instruments and two interviews created for the trial. Pre- and postrelease social support was measured with four standardized instruments and two interviews created for the trial. Eight other psychosocial constructs as well as participant satisfaction with the intervention were assessed with a total of 10 other standardized instruments and four qualitative and semistructured surveys. To locate assessment tools, the PI searched the *Alcohol and Drug Institute* of the University of Washington, the *Institute of Behavioral Research* at Texas Christian University, the *Mental Measurements Yearbook; Health and Psychosocial Instruments,* and instruments used by other studies with similar goals and criminal justice populations.

LOOKING AHEAD

Because of the extensiveness of the *Support Matters* trial, the PI did not start her proposed research agenda with the DOC with this trial. Instead, the PI started with a much smaller preliminary cross-sectional study that involved only two prisons and two community supervision agencies. This approach allowed the PI and the DOC to get to know one another and to gradually plan for a much larger randomized controlled trial. During this process, the PI also became familiar with DOC's research proposal approval process. Because the length of the research approval process at DOC is similar to the length of the university approval process, the PI chose to work simultaneously with the DOC and university human subject review board members. In some cases, it will be best to obtain approval from the university before contacting the DOC or vice versa. Because the PI worked with each entity simultaneously, she had to ensure that any changes in either application were reflected in the other application. The PI also eventually submitted an approved copy of the university application to the DOC review board.

The mobility of prisoners between state prisons was also an important consideration for the PI for recruitment purposes. The PI needed to understand how far in advance from release the research team could recruit prisoners for a postrelease program. The PI ultimately chose to recruit participants across eight cohorts because this would allow her to maximize her sample size and recruit participants nearest to their release date (thus they would be less likely to move across institutions). Because North Carolina has 70 state prisons, the PI needed to know from which prisons prisoners would most likely be released who were returning to the county of the *Support Matters* trial. The PI worked with the DOC to identify those prisons with the highest number of releases to the trial county per month as well as those prisons with the greatest proximity to that county. Recognizing the interconnectedness of the state prison system and by working with the DOC about prisoner mobility, the PI was also able to recruit from prisons that transfer prisoners among one another. Therefore, if the PI missed a potential participant at one of the prisons, the potential participant could still be recruited from another one of the prison-based research sites.

Because former prisoners are also a highly mobile population in the community, the PI incorporated pre- and postrelease mechanisms to try to reduce attrition of consented participants. Prior to release, study participants completed "locator sheets" in which they listed contact information of friends, family members, and community agencies that could help research team members locate them upon release. At each subsequent community-based data collection point, the participant updated this locator sheet. The PI anticipated that postrelease mobility would be highest within the first 3 months of release. As such, the PI included weekly semistructured interviews with the former prisoners. These interviews collected substance misuse, criminal behavior, and social support data and also helped the research team member to stay in contact with study participants. These interviews were reduced to 3 week intervals after the first 3 months of the postrelease period. The interviews only took about 5 minutes to complete and could be conducted in person or over the phone. Treatment and control group participants received $5 remunerations for each of the interviews. For all interviews, the remunerations were equal for treatment and control participants to reduce the likelihood of differential attrition.

RACE AND ETHNICITY ISSUES

Because *Support Matters* was a pilot trial, the PI wanted to assess the characteristics of those former prisoners who would be most likely to participate in the intervention. For this reason, the PI used a census sampling approach rather than stratified sampling. Stratified sampling would have better ensured a sample that was representative of the various race and ethnicity characteristics of the North Carolina prison population. The DOC has a significant percentage of Latino prisoners. Because the PI was not equipped to deliver the intervention or research instruments in Spanish, only English-speaking prisoners were eligible for participation. This approach is a limitation of the trial and did not allow the PI to test the intervention with a large and growing portion of the prison population. The PI was required to address this limitation in all grant and research approval applications. In these applications, the PI identified a plan for incorporating non-English-speaking participants in future applications of the trial. When possible, researchers should accommodate non-English speaking participants in their initial trials.

IMPLEMENTING *SUPPORT MATTERS*

As discussed earlier, the timing of project start up can be complicated in criminal justice field-based research. The PI initially planned to begin recruitment for the *Support Matters* trial in July. However, during that same time period the DOC closed six prisons. The prison closures affected movement and operations among almost all of the state prison systems. The prison closures led to delays in *Support Matters* recruitment. Initially, the PI knew the final approval for recruitment to begin was delayed, but was not notified of the reason for the delay. Because of the PI's initial relationship-building work, she was able to find out quickly the reason for the delay and establish a more realistic timeframe for recruitment, which turned out to be October. The PI used this time to conduct a trial run of the intervention in the community with volunteers who represented the characteristics of the study population. The PI also used the time to redesign her training protocols for the research team members and the practitioners who would deliver the intervention.

The *Support Matters* trial included recruitment from 10 prisons over the period of a year. As a result, the PI needed "buy-in" from each prison. Although all of the prisons were governed by the overarching state DOC entity, each prison had variations in organizational culture and operations. Prisons also varied in the custody level of the prison population (e.g., minimum, medium, maximum), the types of services or programs that are offered to the prison population, and the age range of the prisoners. The PI traveled to each prison and met with top administrators and line staff in advance of starting participant recruitment. The purposes of the meetings were as much relational as they were functional. The meeting agenda began with a project overview, the reason the prison was selected, and the broad implications for that prison. Specific meeting agenda items included identification of primary contact persons for the study, the study window and recruitment of participants, logistics of participant interviewing, and any questions or concerns of the prison officials about the project. The PI addressed organizational culture issues during these meetings including the staff's comfort with research projects, dress code, and formal and informal expectations around the best time to be in the prison doing recruitment.

HUMAN SUBJECTS ISSUES

The PI's preliminary study with the DOC familiarized her with the basic procedures required of both the DOC and the university. However, the *Support Matters* trial involved far more human subjects considerations. As mentioned earlier, the PI worked with the DOC research board and the university research board simultaneously. The PI communicated with the DOC research board via email and over the phone. The PI also met with DOC representatives in person before submitting an application. During this meeting, the PI reviewed the *Support Matters* program (including bringing the representatives a copy of the program treatment manual) and the PI's expectations for the trial. The PI focused the meeting on obtaining feedback from the DOC and brainstorming potential solutions to any concerns about program and research protocols. The PI was then able to address these concerns and include approaches that had been suggested in the meeting in the final research application to the DOC as well as to the university.

Prior to submitting the research proposal to the human subject's review board, the PI asked colleagues to review the application. However, first, the PI reviewed other similar research to assess how researchers addressed key safety and coercion issues in prior studies. The PI also reviewed her previous research applications at her current institution and previous universities in order to make sure she had addressed key concerns. Finally, she contacted the university review board Chair and asked him specific questions in advance and made sure to address these questions in her application. Because the PI had worked closely with the DOC about the research proposal, she had already met with the university's criminal justice representative. This was a matter of chance. The university's criminal justice representative will not always be affiliated with the DOC in general, or necessarily be a part of the DOC review board team.

DEVELOPING THE PROJECT TEAM

The research team and practitioner training (herein referred to as the project team) included a heavy emphasis on educating the team members about the characteristics of the population and the importance of, and nuances of, RCTs. The PI shortened the length of training sessions (i.e., 2 hours instead of 4) and extended the training sessions over several weeks. The training started with obtaining an understanding of project team members' perceptions of prisoners and the prison system. The PI then provided the project team with research-based information related to their perceptions. Next the PI reviewed the empirical literature and theoretical foundation of the *Support Matters* trial with the project team members. The PI then conducted two training sessions on why researchers conduct RCTs and threats to external and internal validity that can occur when such RCTs are conducted in community-based settings. Finally, the PI created a DVD of a mock trial of *Support Matters* in which project team members acted as *Support Matters* participants and the PI delivered the intervention. This allowed the PI to model the program and allowed the project team members to experience the intervention from a participant's perspective.

CONCLUSIONS

The case example demonstrates successful implementation of a field research project and describes how strategies outlined above were approached in one study. Field research within criminal justice settings can be a lengthy and complicated process with a myriad of unique human subjects considerations. As a result, some social workers may perceive human subjects issues and other logistics as insurmountable and thus avoid research with criminal justice-involved populations. In this chapter we counter this perception by providing concrete strategies to conducting field research in criminal justice settings. We indicate that the extant literature is particularly lacking in appropriate measurement instruments and intervention research that is theoretically driven and includes fidelity and assessment tools. Because of professional training in multilevel systemic approaches to social problems and vulnerable populations, social workers are well positioned to make important contributions to U.S. society's understanding of, and response to, those who become criminally involved.

ADDITIONAL READINGS

Center for Advancing Correctional Excellence. (2011). *Center for advancing correctional excellence: Criminology, law, & society.* George Mason University. http://www.gmuace.org/.

Center for Criminal Justice Research. (2011). *Excellence in criminal justice research.* University of Cincinnati. http://www.uc.edu/ccjr/.

Nellis, A., Greene, J., & Mauer, M. (2008). *Reducing racial disparity in the criminal justice system: A manual for practitioners and policymakers.* The Sentencing Project. http://www.sentencingproject.org/doc/publications/rd_reducingracialdisparity.pdf.

Pettus, C. A., & Severson, M. (2006). Paving the way for effective reentry practice: The critical role and function of the boundary spanner. *The Prison Journal, 86,* 206–229.

Social Work and Criminal Justice. (2011). *Social work and criminal justice: Research, education, innovation.* http://sw-cj.org.

5

Using Extant Research on Adults

INTRODUCTION

As with juveniles, there are numerous extant data sets that have been collected by seasoned university-based and nonuniversity-based researchers
that are available. These data collections, usually funded by the federal
government and/or private foundations, contain a wide variety of data of
interest to researchers who study adults and the criminal justice system.
Although providing a unique and rich resource for conducting theory-
testing and descriptive studies, these data sources often present many
challenges.

This chapter will describe the advantages and considerations involved
in using extant research data on adults, suggest techniques to overcome
commonly encountered problems when using these types of data, and
discuss the critical issue of dissemination. Guidance on how data are
deposited in major repositories, such as the Inter-University Consortium
for Political and Social Research (ICPSR), and on how to access these
data files can be found in Chapter 2 and are not repeated here. To further
enhance the use of extant research data an annotated bibliography of
available data files and additional readings is provided.

Types of data available for adults are highly varied. Numerous data
sets contain data on past imprisonment, parole and probation, history of

violence and antisocial behavior, and childhood histories of problem behavior. Some data sets are clearly collected with the express purpose of answering research questions about adults in the criminal justice system. However, as is the case with data on juveniles, many data sets contain a wealth of information, yet there is no indication from the title of the data set that many of these variables are contained within the file. One of many examples of this is the National Epidemiologic Survey on Alcohol and Related Conditions (NESARC). The NESARC is a nationally representative sample of 43,093 noninstitutionalized U.S. residents aged 18 years and older (Grant, Moore, & Kaplan, 2003). The survey, designed to be the largest comorbidity survey ever conducted, gathered background data and extensive information about substance use and comorbid mental health disorders from individuals living in households and group settings such as shelters, college dormitories, and group homes in all 50 states and the District of Columbia. There are numerous variables in the NESARC pertaining to a wide variety of criminal and antisocial behaviors and history of incarceration. Several papers have been published using these variables (see Vaughn et al., 2009, 2010). Judging from the title of the data and even the brief description provided there would be little reason to believe that these data could be useful to criminal justice researchers.

As with many extant data sets that are nationally representative, the NESARC employed a complex sampling design. Specifically with respect to the NESARC, a multistage cluster sampling design was employed, oversampling young adults, Hispanics, and African-Americans in the interest of obtaining a reliable statistical estimation in these subpopulations and of ensuring appropriate representation of racial/ethnic subgroups. Multistage cluster sampling is commonly used when attempting to provide nationally representative estimates. This is because interviewing all participants is not feasible, so larger units (i.e., clusters) are identified and smaller units are randomly selected from. With respect to the NESARC, the multiple stages of sampling are as follows: 709 primary sampling units (PSUs) provided by the Census Supplementary Survey were selected (stage one). Within the sample PSUs, households were systematically selected (stage two). Finally, individuals (stage three) age 18 years or older were randomly selected from each household (see Grant, Hasin, Chou, Stinson, & Dawson, 2004; Grant et al., 2004). Multistage sampling has the advantage of yielding survey data that are representative of the national population and is therefore potentially strong in yielding findings that have high external validity or generalizability. Despite these advantages, the depth of measurement is often compromised.

The ICPSR is a great place to start searching for extant data files on adults. ICPSR maintains much of the federal data sets on victimization and criminality (e.g., those for the Bureau of Justice Statistics, violence against women data, and the Substance Abuse and Mental Health Data Archive). Also, a relatively new longitudinal study with important criminal justice-related variables is the Fragile Families Study (http://www.fragilefamilies.princeton.edu/about.asp).

As shown in Chapter 2, identifying and accessing data are relatively straightforward. However, this is just the beginning as learning what questions were asked, the question response formats, the frequencies of variables that are of interest, as well as understanding how the data were collected so that the design can be incorporated into the analyses; these are all fundamental steps in producing useful reports from these data files. In conjunction with these steps, as discussed in Chapter 2, locating previously published works [searching based on the study principal investigator (PI) and looking at study website bibliographies are good starting points] based on these data files is also essential for several reasons. First, reading these articles provides a shortcut to understanding how other researchers have used the data and particular variables. Second, it shows what has previously been published, so repeating the research is avoided. Third, these works provide insights on the types of analyses that are feasible and often help to generate research questions by learning from what others have done and identifying gaps or possible extensions in prior studies.

One disadvantage of using extant data explicitly collected for criminal justice research is that it is frequently analyzed by the other disciplines such as political scientists and criminologists. However, social workers have a unique contribution to make by asking questions that are specifically related to practice refinement or intervention development.

Some Cautionary Notes Regarding Measurement

Most of the available data on crime and justice have limitations that are often ignored or glossed over. As David Greenberg (2010) has aptly pointed out, "Crime rates are computed only when victims report an offense to the police and they record it. Self-reports of crime are usually unverifiable, and arrests or convictions decisions by criminal justice personnel may distort underlying patterns of crime." Of course, this is not to suggest existing data sources are useless and completely biased as this is not the case, but only that measurement error is alive and well and will not easily go away.

With respect to self-reports of crime, studies consistently find moderate correlations between self-reports of crime and official arrest records (Hindelang, Hirschi, & Weis, 1981; Thornberry & Krohn, 2003). Self-reports have a number of obvious advantages, such as gaining information about behavior that is not detected by law enforcement, efficiency, and allowing researchers to design and ask particular questions. As such, self-report data will likely be around for a long time.

Another significant problem in criminal justice research is the multiple definitions of recidivism, the measure most commonly used to assess desistance from crime. Recidivism is variously defined as commitment of another crime or return to criminal justice supervision. Commitment of another crime can be measured as self-reported offenses, arrest records, and reappearance under criminal justice supervision. Return to criminal justice supervision may happen because a person committed a new crime or because a person violated a condition of criminal justice supervision and was required to remain under supervision or sentenced to more intensive supervision such as prison. Scholars analyzing extant data files should be keenly attuned to the strengths and weaknesses of the various measures used to collect the data they are interested in analyzing.

In addition, computing internal consistency reliability of scales and assessing whether measures are related to constructs they are theoretically supposed to be related to (convergent validity) or not related to (divergent validity), there are other measurement strategies that can be employed to examine the validity of measures in an extant data file. One simple method is to research the history of a given measure with respect to its psychometric properties. For example, did other studies using this measure come to similar conclusions? Is the measure correlated with constructs with which it is suppose to be correlated?

Although many statistical techniques such as exploratory and confirmatory factor analysis, test–retest reliability, and interrater agreement are fundamental tests to be aware of, technique-wise, item response theory modeling and associated assessments of differential item functioning are gaining currency as a rigorous means to examine question validity. The central feature of these techniques is the assessment of question items with respect to differences in the probabilities of endorsing particular items (Cohen, Kim, & Baker, 1993). For example, do adult offenders of relatively the same abilities but from different groups respond differently to specific items examining verbal abilities? If differences are found, further inspection of items may reveal that they are related to a particular underlying dimension such as cognitive understanding (in keeping with the verbal ability example) and thus this knowledge helps to improve and refine these assessments.

Some Practical Advice Regarding Statistical Methods

In Chapter 2 we provided a checklist of data examination strategies with respect to analyzing extant data sets. Here we offer some practical suggestions with respect to employing some commonly and uncommonly used multivariate techniques. Once your research question(s) or study aims are established it is critical to clearly assess how your outcome or dependent variable is measured. Knowing this will determine what analyses can be chosen. For example, if your dependent variable is continuous in nature (as a guideline 10 or more values) then a linear regression model may be warranted. However, criminal justice outcomes are often counts, so Poisson or negative binomial regression is often indicated. Criminal justice data are often available in the form of categories. Categorical dependent variables or outcomes necessitate binary (two categories such as yes or no) or multinomial (three categories such as east, west, north, or south) or ordered (never, sometimes, always) logistic regression. It is helpful to think of your statistical model as embodying your theoretical framework guiding your study. What this means is that variables should represent theoretical constructs. This helps to choose just enough variables needed in a model. Otherwise, model building becomes a poorly guided exercise whereby variables are added on a somewhat ad hoc basis. As such, it is difficult to determine what is being tested. We also realize that statistical model building is often far more exploratory in practice than many researchers are willing to admit. Often induction and exploration can lead to interesting findings or provide new ideas. One practice we often observe among students and researchers is the tendency to believe in a given relationship between constructs or wish to see a given program or intervention work. Although often well intentioned, it is important to note that it is bad scientific practice to work in a way that attempts to prove that a theory or intervention is correct or to verify that a hypothesis is right. Sometimes results are not aligned with our values or ideological biases and as such researchers need to be aware of confirmatory bias.

DISSEMINATION

The issue of dissemination is often overlooked yet is very important. A study may be interesting in its goals, rigorous in its execution, elegant in its statistical analysis, and important in its implications, however this is all for naught if project findings are not properly disseminated to funding entities, scientists, and practitioners. After all, research findings are not very useful if they do not reach their intended audience. The intended audience differs widely. For example, researchers may analyze criminal justice data for the sole purpose of producing a report to influence state or local policy-makers. This type of report should be user friendly, free of jargon, and present a minimum number of fancy statistical analyses or if so they should be presented in a "friendly" manner that policy-makers can readily understand. This contrasts with standard peer-reviewed articles in the social sciences whereby transparencies involving research design and statistical techniques need to be carefully elucidated with some journals often expecting the actual statistical equations to be presented.

The need to prioritize publication efforts is critical. Most datasets offer a multitude of possibilities in terms of publication. When approaching the use of a dataset it is often inefficient to employ the file for just one article. Given the complexity and time it takes to understand and begin analyzing an extant data source it makes sense to do more than one publication with it. Many scholars have built their careers on using one data source. Many times initial papers must be written to satisfy funders or in more elegant terms directly flow from the study aims. In short, initial papers should be the most substantively important. However, there is also value in doing your first paper with an extant source on a less important topic as a way to initiate yourself with a data source (a sort of "trial run"). Some researchers also choose to write papers that will appeal to a large number of journal publication outlets. This strategy enhances the likelihood of eventual publication of findings. Almost invariably, extant data sources are used to answer key research questions. Well-designed studies using extant data sources also include a set of explicit null and/or directional hypotheses to be formally tested in an effort to answer important research questions. This is not to say that exploratory analyses should not be undertaken. As previously alluded to, sometimes the best work is done when finding unexpected relationships in a data source. Some refer to this practice in a derogatory fashion such as "fishing about," but this practice is often useful to get to know the data better and to generate ideas. But when doing so one must be aware that significant associations are not in and of themselves meaningful. It should be remembered that the scientific process is iterative, meaning that theory, data, deduction, and induction are critically intertwined elements informing one another.

Major papers, if sufficiently rigorous, should be targeted to top-tier journals. Although journal impact factor is an important consideration, some journals are flagship journals for a scholarly society in which researchers want to make their mark and have large circulations. Thus, the researcher's overall long-term agenda plays a role in these decisions.

Again, this is an issue of targeting an audience and not one of merely looking to see what journal has the highest impact factor. For example, the journal *Social Work* has a circulation size in excess of 160,000 but a journal impact factor that typically ranges from 0.8 to 1.0. This peculiar situation is likely due to the nature of the *Social Work* readership, which is predominately comprised of master's-level practitioners who may or may not apply the findings to their professional practices, but who generally do not subsequently cite the articles they read. Comparisons of journal impact factors across disciplinary fields can be misleading. Some fields such as biomedicine and health sciences often have higher impact factors for their journals than the social sciences. This is partly due to the fact that these journals reach larger audiences, have a higher density of researchers, and articles are published at a faster rate (Howard & Vaughn, 2008). Because journal impact factors are based on the number of times a given article is cited within a 2-year time frame (some journals are now showing their 5-year impact factor), this facilitates a higher value.

Researchers should take steps to ensure that the substantive focus of their work, theoretical constructs employed, research design, and formatting of the article are suitable for the specific journal being considered for submission. As is the case with getting to know your data, there is also no substitute for getting to know a wide set of journals. A good practice is to examine the most recent 2 to 3 years of issues of all journal publication outlets in your areas of interest. This endeavor can reveal many nuances in the preferences of these journals, such as popular theoretical constructs, concepts being debated, and preferred methodologies. This also provides a nice introduction to some of the current debates in a field, can help generate ideas for future papers, and can provide useful demonstrations of various methodological techniques.

For ethical and practical reasons researchers should acknowledge all persons, groups, and organizations that have contributed to a given publication. It is an especially good idea to acknowledge the funding source that supported the data collection from which the article is written. Although using extant data sources is complex and not without a number of pitfalls, researchers should always bear in mind that they are benefitting from those persons and organizations that designed, collected, and funded the study.

CONCLUSIONS

Using extant data files to study adults is an efficient approach that capitalizes on these rich and powerful sources of information. These data files are typically free or can be obtained by request. And external funding to analyze extant data files is available from major funders such as the National Institutes of Health and Department of Justice. Despite the wide use of these data sources much of it is unused. Exploring these data sets is often useful as no single researcher can collect these large data sets. Taking the time to do so will often lead to new ideas applicable to future data collections.

ADDITIONAL READING

Meyers, L. S., Gamst, G., & Guarino, A. J. (2006). *Applied multivariate research: Design and interpretation.* Thousand Oaks: CA. Sage Press.

ANNOTATED BIBLIOGRAPHY OF DATA SOURCES

The following bibliography describes numerous research data sets that are publicly available. Although not an exhaustive list, it does provide a variety of data sources from which important questions can (and have been) asked. Because new data sets are continually being added, researchers should explore ICPSR to identify data sets for their specific needs.

Project on Human Development in Chicago Neighborhoods (PHDCN) Series, 1995–2002

   Sample Size/Population: Chicago residents comprising 8782 adults
   Time: 1995–2002

Assessments: Two surveys using systematic social observation (SSO) techniques were done on 343 Chicago neighborhood blocks (n = 8782 adults), as well 2 longitudinal studies. The longitudinal studies examined subjects' lives and their shifting environmental conditions in regard to antisocial behaviors.

Survey of Texas Adults

Sample Size/Population: Texas adults age 18 years and over

Time: 2004

Assessments: A random-digit dialing sample with questions pertaining to civic engagement, personality, violence, physical/mental health status, religion, and demographic information.

Census of State and Federal Adult Correctional Facilities

Sample Size/Population: 957 state prison facilities, 250 state community-based facilities, and 80 federal prisons operating in June 29, 1990

Time: 1990 (other times include 1974, 1979, and 1984)

Assessments: Self-enumerated questionnaires regarding prison facilities, demographic make-up of incarcerated adults, drug incidents, drug policies, as well as drug treatment and intervention programs.

Physical Violence in American Families

Sample Size/Population: Adults in American families (currently married or living together; or single parents with children under 18 years in the household, or had been married or had lived with a partner of the opposite sex within the past 2 years)

Time: 1985

Assessments: Demographic variables such as age, race, sex, employment status, etc.

Criminal Violence and Incapacitation in California, 1962–1988

Sample Size/Population: Adult men released from California prisons between 1962 and 1988 (original sample size 6000; attrition sample size was 4897)

Time: 1962–1988

Assessments: Looked at the usefulness of statistical methods (multiple-regression analysis) in predicting recidivism.

Violent Offending by Drug Users: Longitudinal Arrest Histories
of Adults Arrested in Washington, DC, 1985–1986

Sample Size/Population: Stratified random sample of adult arrestees in Washington, DC (based on arrest record for any charge)

Time: 1985–1986

Assessments: Longitudinal arrest data were gathered to characterize violent offending of drug and nondrug users.

Domestic Violence and Substance Abuse Among the Arrestee
Population in Albuquerque, New Mexico

Sample Size/Population: 696 persons booked and arrested on local and state charges in Bernalillo County, New Mexico

Time: 1999–2001

Assessments: Looked at domestic violence among intimate partners within an arrestee population using the National Institute of Justice's ADAM (Arrestee Drug Abuse Monitoring) program.

Alcohol Availability, Type of Alcohol Establishment, Distribution
Policies, and Their Relationship to Crime and Disorder
in the District of Columbia, 2000–2006

Sample Size/Population: 431 of the 433 block groups in Washington, DC

Time: 2000–2006

Assessments: Assessed the relationship between alcohol availability and violence and disorder. The study developed a GIS (geographic information system) containing crime, demographic characteristics, and physical characteristics.

Operation and Structure of Right-Wing Extremist Groups in the United
States, 1980–2007

Sample Size/Population: 112 persons from 16 RWE (right-wing extremist groups)

Time: 1980–2007

Assessments: Compared right-wing extremist "advocates" with "implementers" and identified recruitment patterns among each group.

Outcome Evaluation of the Residential Substance Abuse Treatment (RSAT) Program for State Prisoners in Massachusetts, 1999–2002
    Sample Size/Population: 188 inmates referred to the RSAT program at Barnstable County House of Corrections, Massachusetts who met chronic offender status
    Time: 1999–2002
    Assessments: Outcome evaluation of the RSAT program.

Uniform Crime Reporting Program Data (United States) Series
    Sample Size/Population: Reported crimes that are not available elsewhere within the criminal justice system
    Time: 1929–present
    Assessments: ICPSR archives the Uniform Crime Reporting (UCR) data as five separate components: summary data, county-level data, incident-level data, hate crime data, and various, mostly nonrecurring, data collections.

Annual Survey of Jails in Indian Country Series
    Sample Size/Population: Adults and Juveniles in Indian reservations, pueblos, Rancherias, and other Native American and Alaska Native communities throughout the United States
    Time: 1998 to present
    Assessments: The survey provides data on inmates, staffing, and facility characteristics, as well as the needs of all confinement facilities operated by tribal authorities or the Bureau of Indian Affairs (BIA).

Annual Survey of Jails
    Sample Size/Population: Adult and juvenile U.S. inmate populations
    Time: 1982 to present
    Assessments: Every 5 to 6 years, census data on the full size of the jail population and selected inmate characteristics are obtained.

Arrestee Drug Abuse Monitoring (ADAM) Program/Drug Use Forecasting (DUF) Series
    Sample Size/Population: 1987–1997 included 24 sites across the United States from U.S. criminals arrested and booked (number of sites varied from year to year). Juvenile data were added in 1991. In 2000, the sites were increased to 35 cities, only looking at adult populations of

arrestees. Note: The data represent only the number of arrests, as opposed to an unduplicated count of persons arrested.

Time: 1987–1997, 2000 to present

Assessments: The DUF program was designed to estimate the prevalence of drug use and detect changes in trends in drug use among U.S. persons arrested and booked. Arrestees supplied self-report measures and urine samples. (Urine samples were screened for 10 illicit drugs.) Note: In 2000, the ADAM program, redesigned from the DUF program, moved to a probability-based sampling for only the adult male population.

Census of State and Federal Adult Correctional Facilities Series

Sample Size/Population: Federal and state-operated adult confinement and correctional facilities within the United States

Time: Ongoing; produced every 5 years

Assessments: Data variables include, but are not limited to, physical security, capital and operating expenditures, custody level of residents/inmates, race/ethnicity of inmates, inmate deaths, and assaults and incidents by inmates.

National Addiction and HIV Data Archive Program (NAHDAP)
Criminal Justice Drug Abuse Treatment Studies (CJ-DATS)
1. Performance Indicators for Corrections (PIC)

Sample Size/Population: Over 3000 participants from various correctional sites

Time: 2002–2008

Assessments: Evaluates clients functioning and treatment participation, as well as client responses to treatment intervention.

2. Targeted Interventions for Corrections (TIC)

Sample Size/Population: Male/female respondents, 18 years or older, from various drug treatment programs for offenders in each of the correctional facilities

Time: 2002–2008

Assessments: Measures the effects of treatment programs in criminal justice settings in order to establish an evidence-based library of targeted treatment interventions.

National Crime Victimization Survey (NCVS) Series
Sample Size/Population: Cluster samples of U.S. victims, 12 and older
Time: Ongoing
Assessments: NCVS provides detailed information about the victims and consequences of crime, estimates the number and classification of crimes not reported to police, and provides measures of selected types of crime.

National Health and Nutritional Examination Survey
(NHANES) and Follow-up Series
Sample Size/Population: Cluster samples of civilian noninstitutionalized U.S. residents with high risks for malnutrition, ages 2 months to 74 years
Time: 1959–1984 (Four-Part Series)
Assessments: The NHANES I Epidemiologic Follow-up Study (NHEFS) is a longitudinal study designed to investigate the relationships between clinical, nutritional, and behavioral factors. NHANES II (1976–1980) was designed to continue the measurement and monitoring of the nutritional status and health of the U.S. population. NHANES III (1988–1994) contains information on a sample of 33,994 persons aged 2 months and older. The Hispanic HANES (HHANES) was conducted to obtain sufficient numbers to produce estimates of the health and nutritional status of Hispanics, as well as specific data for Puerto Ricans, Mexican-Americans, and Cuban-Americans.

National Incident-Based Reporting System (NIBRS) Series
Sample Size/Population: U.S. criminal population
Time: Late 1970s to present
Assessments: Comprehensive data on each single incident and arrest based on 22 offense categories made up of 46 specific crimes. The series also collects arrest data on 11 minor offense categories.

National Jail Census Series
Sample Size/Population: U.S. jail population, both juvenile and adult (excludes federal and/or state administered facilities, as well as jail-prison systems in Alaska, Connecticut, Delaware, Hawaii, Rhode Island, and Vermont)

Time: Every 5 years (most recent 2006)

Assessments: Data include jail population by reason being held, age and sex, etc.

National Longitudinal Surveys (NLS) Series

Sample Size/Population: Five groups of Americans: older men aged 45–59, mature women aged 30–44, young men aged 14–24, young women aged 14–24, and youths aged 14–21 years, as well as children born to mothers within the survey

Time: 1960s to present (Youth: 1979 to present); (Children: 1986 to present)

Assessments: A set of longitudinal surveys relating to the labor market experiences of five specific groups of American men and women. The data also include cognitive-socioemotional-physiological assessments administered to NLSY mothers and their children. Note: The Bureau of Labor Statistics website contains the most current data for this series.

State Court Statistics Series

Sample Size/Population: State appellate and trial court caseloads by type of case for the 50 states, District of Columbia, and Puerto Rico

Time: Ongoing annually

Assessments: Major areas of investigation include case filings, case dispositions, and appellate opinions. Case types include civil cases, capital punishment cases, other criminal cases, juvenile cases, administrative agency appeals, and several other types.

Criminal Violence and Incapacitation in California

Sample Size/Population: 6310 men in California prisons in the early 1960s with a follow-up study consisting of 4897 men (omits those men from the original 6310 lost to attrition).

Time: 1960–1988

Assessments: Examines whether statistical models are useful in predicting recidivism.

Reducing Violent Crimes and Firearms in Indianapolis, Indiana

Sample: 1000 felony probationers convicted of 13 violent, drug, gun, and property offenses

Time: 2003–2005

Assessments: Experimental evaluation of a lever-pulling strategy in Indianapolis, Indiana to deter violent and firearm crimes.

Women Coping in Prison at the Fluvanna Correctional
Center for Women in Virginia

Sample: 802 women convicted of serious felonies in a maximum security prison

Time: 1999–2000

Assessments: Mental health symptoms, personality, coping behaviors, convictions, and impulsivity.

6

Administrative Data on Adults

INTRODUCTION

Similar to the juvenile justice system, administrative data offer considerable opportunities for researchers interested in studying the criminal justice system and individuals processed in it. Entities involved in the criminal justice system collect information about their activities and the individuals who come through their doors. There may be more opportunities, actually, to do research in the criminal justice system using administrative data than in the juvenile justice system. For example, sentencing guidelines have been implemented in many criminal justice systems whereas they are seldom used in the juvenile justice systems. The use of sentencing guidelines means that information relevant to determining the guideline score is systematically collected and can often be used to address a range of research questions that have considerable policy and practice relevance. Furthermore, many corrections departments systematically collect and record data that can be used to answer a range of questions such as the characteristics associated with differences in prison behavior, movement of individuals within the correctional system, variations in the amount of time served in prison and on parole, and factors associated with various postrelease outcomes. Although the location of the information is likely to vary across states, data are often available regarding the experiences and outcomes of individuals on probation and parole or other community-based correctional programs. Therefore there is an excellent opportunity to use administrative data to assess the effectiveness of these programs and services.

Consequently, researchers interested in the criminal justice system should consider the role that administrative data can play in answering a range of questions. This chapter facilitates that process by exploring the role and uses of administrative data for research on the criminal justice system, the advantages and limitations of administrative data, how to build partnerships and gain access to data, human subjects and ethical issues, and strategies for data collection, management, and analysis.

ROLE AND USES OF ADMINISTRATIVE DATA ON ADULTS

Like the juvenile justice system, the criminal justice system is best con- ceptualized as a loosely coupled system in which numerous agencies and actors are engaged in making decisions about individual cases. Each agency and set of actors is charged with specific tasks in the criminal justice process and is often required to collect information pertaining to these tasks. Although agencies and actors involved in the criminal justice system do interact and these interactions can shape how cases are han- dled prior to subsequent decision-making points, it is likely that a given agency is primarily collecting information pertaining to that agency's specific function. In addition to collecting basic information, many of these agencies also collect additional information that helps them to complete this function. The type of information collected varies consid- erably across entities, but often includes information such as

- demographic characteristics,
- arrests and correctional supervision events,
- offense and conviction history,
- risk to reoffend assessments,
- health and psychosocial evaluations,
- correctional program participation (e.g., alcohol and drug),

- risk management classifications, and
- violations of supervision conditions.

Similar to the juvenile justice system, data collected by criminal justice entities are used to develop official records for a variety of reporting and management requirements. Yet a lot of information collected by entities in the criminal justice system is underutilized and can lend itself to addressing a range of research questions. For organizational purposes, we include two broad categories of studies. The first involves the administration of criminal justice. Studies in this category focus on decision making and case processing and in how the criminal justice system handles cases. A great deal of research focusing on the administration of criminal justice focuses on the courts and sentencing structures. For example, researchers have used data from the Pennsylvania Commission on Sentencing to examine the implementation of sentencing guidelines in criminal courts (Kramer & Ulmer, 1996, 2002; Ulmer & Kramer, 1996, 1998), to assess racial and age differences in sentencing (Steffensmeier, Ulmer, & Kramer, 1998; Steffensmeier, Kramer, & Ulmer, 1996), and to assess differences in sentences received by juveniles compared to adults (Kurlychek & Johnson, 2004). These types of studies are important because they aide in understanding how the criminal justice system operates. They also assess potential disparities by race, ethnicity, gender, age, and other characteristics. Consequently, these studies have tremendous relevance for policy and practice and have spurred considerable debate about the criminal justice system.

Studies focusing on the administration of criminal justice, however, are not limited to the courts. Criminal justice officials at the "back end" of the conviction process also have discretion in determining what happens to a particular case. For example, probation and parole officers often have discretion over whether an individual is charged with a technical violation of the terms of their probation or parole. Technical violations can lead to additional sanctions or to an individual being committed to jail or prison. Once in prison, staff can assess "good time" and give prisoners "credits" for good behavior and program participation that will reduce the number of days they are required to serve in prison.

The extent to which these days can be reduced is determined legislatively and/or by judges. Administrative data can be useful for understanding some of these issues and researchers can consider their use as they conceptualize and design studies.

The second category of studies for which administrative data can be useful is focused on the case outcomes of interventions within the criminal justice system. Although the prior category of research using administrative data is well studied by a variety of disciplines, less attention has been given to intervention research with criminal justice-involved cases. Program evaluation studies in the extant literature are limited in number compared to the amount of programming that occurs in prison. There is a particular deficit in research that emphasizes the development of interventions. Administrative data are very useful in providing a preliminary understanding of the effectiveness of correctional interventions and can be used to develop interventions as well as inform more complex research designs. Advanced statistical analysis approaches such as propensity score modeling can also be used to account for some of the limitations (or lack thereof) in research evaluations of existing interventions within the criminal justice system. For example, one project involved collaboration between a research team and state department of correction to evaluate a prison-based sex offender treatment program. Participants volunteer for the program, but not all volunteers receive the program. The Department wanted to understand if volunteerism contributed to posttreatment outcomes. We used propensity score analysis to model factors that may influence volunteerism and thus indirectly influence case outcomes. Study findings have important implications for correctional administrators and intervention researchers.

ADVANTAGES AND LIMITATIONS OF ADMINISTRATIVE DATA IN CRIMINAL JUSTICE

Many of the advantages and limitations of administrative data in the criminal justice system are similar to those in the juvenile justice system. The nature of the entities involved in the criminal justice system is that they collect information on everyone who comes through their doors, meaning that there is the potential to draw large samples. The reality that this information is being collected over time enhances the ability to conduct longitudinal studies and to examine the timing of specific events on outcomes of interest. These studies are also often less expensive and results can be provided more quickly than longitudinal studies utilizing other forms of data collection. Some administrative data may be more reliable because the information is collected within the official capacity of the criminal justice system and is not subject to the recall of an individual during an interview. The utility of administrative data is greater in those situations in which data can be matched across agencies and time (e.g., childhood to adulthood).

Differences between the criminal and juvenile justice systems offer potential advantages that make administrative data with adults appealing. For example, the use of formal structures such as sentencing guidelines means that uniform data are, at least theoretically, being collected across jurisdictions within states regarding such things as sentencing decisions. Furthermore, the structure of the Department of Corrections in many states means that consistent data are being collected across the state with regard to the prisons system and potentially the parole system. This is not often the case in the juvenile system where courts and community supervision offices typically maintain their own data systems and do not often utilize consistent tools in making decisions about how to handle cases. Juvenile residential placements in many states are also likely to be more loosely connected, meaning that it is more difficult to obtain systematic data on a state level.

Many limitations to using administrative data in the adult criminal justice system are similar to those in the juvenile justice system. Researchers need to be aware that often substantial work is associated with getting administrative data files ready for analysis, matching cases across and within agencies, and accounting for data entry error. They also need to be aware that data elements of interest may not be available due to the way that the information was collected, stored, and coded and therefore compromises may be required. Also, the quality of the data may be unclear. Researchers should talk with agency professionals to assess the quality of training and consistency of data entry when using administrative data. As is the case with any study involving the criminal justice system, researchers need to have a firm conceptualization of the study they wish to conduct and the role that administrative data play in the study design. Although administrative data can directly answer some questions, in other cases it is useful to use in conjunction with other types of primary data collection or to generate additional research questions that might involve other types of data collection or lead to intervention studies.

BUILDING PARTNERSHIPS AND GAINING ACCESS TO ADMINISTRATIVE DATA

As discussed in previous chapters, conducting research in the criminal justice system requires a lot of time and effort. Strategies and techniques for building relationships have been covered in depth in previous chapters. Thus, the goal of this section is to briefly reiterate the key points. In essence, successful researchers are able to build partnerships with a variety of actors and are able to work with those actors over time. A large component of building these relationships is to understand the realities of the criminal justice system, the politics of the environment, and the benefits that research can have for the system. Acquiring this understanding requires researchers to do their "homework" prior to engaging with actors and agencies, to use contacts and networks to facilitate relationships within the system, and to be willing to give back to actors and agencies through the research process.

This latter point can be particularly important in building and maintaining relationships within the criminal justice system, particularly for doctoral students or junior faculty members. Most of the time, researchers within academic institutions are focused on peer-reviewed publications as the end result of research projects. This is a requirement of an academic career and researchers need to be continually cognizant of the need to publish. Yet, there are also many results from the analysis of administrative data, as well as other studies in the criminal justice system, that might not necessarily end up in peer-reviewed journals but will inform policy and practice. Furthermore, the format of journal articles, the complexity of statistical techniques, and the time that it takes to get articles published mean that results might be inaccessible to many in the field or that they are not produced in a timely manner. Consequently, it is important for researchers to understand the value of communicating the results of their studies in a variety of ways (e.g., reports, policy or research briefs, presentations, testimony). This can be time consuming, so it is necessary to be careful about the time spent doing so, but it can also be important to the agencies and actors that are providing data or access and can help to establish the legitimacy of the researcher in the system and build long-term relationships.

Another key point to developing and building relationships is the need for patience and planning. As mentioned in other chapters, researchers seeking to study the criminal justice system need to realize that it often takes time to get access to data. Although in some cases it is possible to obtain data quickly, it is often necessary to adjust to delays in gaining entry into the system. Based on these realities, one suggestion is that researchers should think about their long-term research agenda when attempting to build relationships within the criminal justice system. Projects should be focused on those that are obviously relevant to the researchers' interests and needs of the system, but that also have the potential for several publications and additional projects. Doing so can make the time and energy involved in gaining entry into the criminal justice system pay off long-term.

HUMAN SUBJECTS AND ETHICAL ISSUES

As noted previously, research projects using administrative data are often easier to get approved by the Institutional Review Board (IRB) than those involving other types of data collection. An advantage of working in the criminal justice system is that the majority of individuals involved in criminal justice are over the age of 18 years. Although prisoners receive considerable human subjects protections, it is often more difficult to conduct research when dealing with children who are incarcerated or otherwise institutionalized. Like studies using administrative data from the juvenile justice system, studies using administrative data in the criminal justice system are defined as exempt if they are based on preexisting data, documents, or records (i.e., those that are currently in existence) and do not contain any identifying information. This means that if an agency is willing to provide its data without identifiable information, the study is exempt from IRB review and many studies using administrative data fall within this category. When seeking to match data, an honest broker can be used as the intermediary between the researcher and individuals being studied. The honest broker must be someone who is not involved in the research and has legitimate access to the data.

Many criminal justice agencies will also have an IRB process and researchers should understand these requirements because they might delay the project. When the data contain identifying information, the study cannot be defined as exempt and the researcher must go through the typical review process. This can get complicated and we refer you to earlier discussions (Chapters 1 and 4) to learn more about how to navigate the IRB to conduct research in the juvenile justice system and field research in the criminal justice system. Because each situation will differ, we highly recommend working with your institutional IRB to plan your study and determine what you need to do to comply with human subjects protections.

DATA COLLECTION, MANAGEMENT, AND ANALYSIS

The most important aspect of collecting administrative data is for the researcher to be clear in what he or she is requesting. Sometimes, this is facilitated by codebooks or other descriptions of the types of information that are available, but many times codebooks are not available. Often, this process occurs over a period of time and through conversations with key actors within an agency. The researcher needs to be prepared with enough detail about what he or she is looking for and to ask appropriate questions of the entity. Working with someone within the information management or research department is typically necessary because these are the people who are most likely to understand what information is being collected and how it is being collected. This process is likely to take time, especially if the request is complex or requires data from various agencies or departments. It is also likely that when the researcher gains access to the data it will take considerable time to get it ready for analysis. For example, a file may contain multiple lines of data for each individual and multiple files may be necessary to obtain the data elements of interest. Researchers should plan for the time that it takes to work with these files and for the potential that they will need help in doing so. They should also plan on needing to work with the agency to fully understand the structure of the file and the meaning and quality of data elements.

CONCLUSIONS

Administrative data are used for a variety of functions including understanding the process of the criminal justice system, the trajectories of its cases, and the outcomes of interventions within the system. Administrative data are a remarkable research resource and are perhaps most efficiently used when matched with other types of data collection or as preliminary studies for applied investigations. The use of administrative data provides near endless opportunities for answering pressing research questions and social work researchers would be well advised to take advantage of this drastically underutilized resource.

ADDITIONAL RESOURCES

Hagan, F. E. (2005). *Essentials of research methods in criminal justice and criminology.* Boston, MA: Pearson/Allyn & Bacon.

Joyce, P. (2009). *Criminology and criminal justice: A study guide.* Portland, OR: Willan Publishing.

King, R. D., & Wincup, E. (Eds.) (2008). *Doing research on crime and justice.* New York: Oxford University Press.

Appendix 1

Stages of Formulating a Justice-Based Research-Based Project

Stages of Development	Field Research	Extant Data	Administrative Data
Stage 1	Develop research in partnership with criminal justice agency.	Conceptualize broad research interests.	Reach out to people within the professional network who have relationships with justice agencies.
	Agree upon a mutually beneficial research project.	Identify possible data repositories and data sets.	Identify key stakeholders.
Stage 2	Identify research questions.	Identify specific research questions.	Seek understanding of the local or state justice environment.
	Define constructs to answer research question.	Become familiar with prior studies conducted on similar concepts.	Identify all possible sources/agencies of data.

(Continued)

Stages of Development	Field Research	Extant Data	Administrative Data
	Ask partners how they measure the related constructs.	Review prior studies conducted with the data set of interest.	Seek out partnerships across relevant agencies.
	Determine how to adequately account for race and ethnic diversity.	When applicable, contact the principal investigator of the given data set.	Determine if an "honest broker" is needed.
Stage 3	Assess the timeline for human subject applications.	Review data set sampling procedures and codebook.	Develop a clear conceptualization of research interest.
	Request feedback from partners timing for project start up.	Assess how other authors have defined variables.	Select a mutually beneficial research project.
	Understand client mobility.		
Stage 4	Address logistical barriers to data collection with key stakeholders.	Understand the distributional characteristics of variables.	Specify key constructs necessary to answering the research questions.
	Determine organizational culture dynamics relevant to research implementation.	Determine an appropriate dissemination plan.	Work with partners to determine how the constructs are measured and where the data are stored.
Stage 5	Begin thinking about a dissemination plan.	Match researcher goals with publication outlet.	Contact the University Institutional Review Board (IRB) to discuss the application.
	Train the research team.		Work with partner IRB as appropriate.

Appendix 2

Flow Chart of the Juvenile and Criminal Justice System in the United States

What is the sequence of events in the criminal justice system?

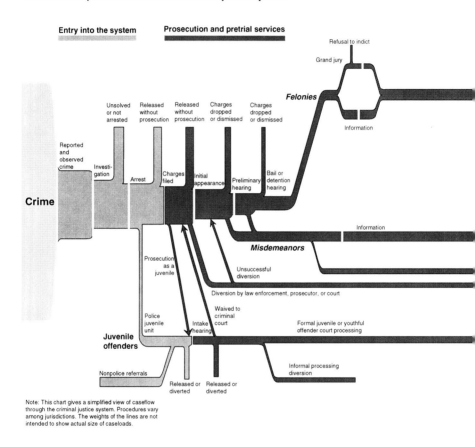

Note: This chart gives a simplified view of caseflow through the criminal justice system. Procedures vary among jurisdictions. The weights of the lines are not intended to show actual size of caseloads.

Chart from the Bureau of Justice Statistics
http://bjs.ojp.usdoj.gov/content/largechart.cfm#

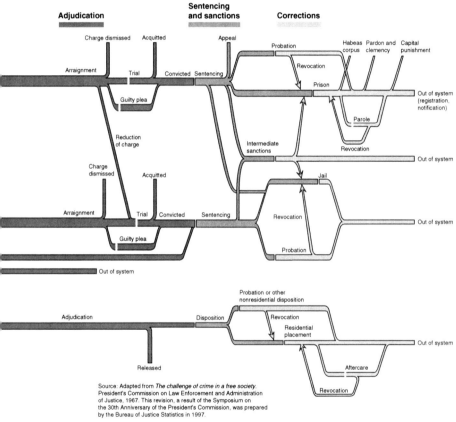

Adjudication

Sentencing and sanctions

Corrections

Source: Adapted from *The challenge of crime in a free society*, President's Commission on Law Enforcement and Administration of Justice, 1967. This revision, a result of the Symposium on the 30th Anniversary of the President's Commission, was prepared by the Bureau of Justice Statistics in 1997.

Appendix 3

Essential Components in Human Subjects Applications

✓ Purpose and rationale for a study usually including a literature review.
✓ Research questions and study aims.
✓ Detailed sample description.
   ○ Inclusion and exclusion criteria.
✓ Full description of the study.
   ○ Study design.
      ▪ For an extant and administrative study, full description of existing data including how the data were collected and stored.
   ○ Methods for identifying and/or recruiting study participants.
      ▪ Procedures for obtaining participant consent.
      ▪ Costs to participants/partnering agency.
      ▪ Inducement for study participants.
   ○ Detailed description of what participants will be asked to do as applicable.
      ▪ Includes frequency and duration of contact.
   ○ Study measures.
      ▪ Data collection points.
      ▪ Psychometric properties.

- ✓ Benefits of the study to participants and to society.
- ✓ Risks to participants (and research team as applicable).
  - ○ Discussion of how risks will be identified and measures taken to reduce those risks.
- ✓ Data collection and analysis plan.
- ✓ Participant identifiers.
- ✓ Confidentiality plan.
- ✓ Data sharing plan.
- ✓ Data security for storage and transmission.

Appendix 4

Resources

Agency for Healthcare Research and Quality
  http://www.ahrq.gov/
Alcohol and Drug Abuse Institute
  http://depts.washington.edu/adai/
Behavior Data Systems
  http://www.bdsltd.com/
Bureau of Justice Statistics
  http://bjs.ojp.usdoj.gov/
Campbell Collaboration
  http://www.campbellcollaboration.org/
Center for Court Innovation
  http://www.courtinnovation.org
Centers for Disease Control and Prevention
  http://www.cdc.gov
The Criminal Justice/Mental Health Consensus Project
  http://consensusproject.org
The Fragile Families and Child Wellbeing Study
  http://www.fragilefamilies.princeton.edu/
Institute of Behavioral Research—Texas Christian University
  http://www.ibr.tcu.edu/pubs/datacoll/listofforms.html

Inter-university Consortium for Political and Social Research
http://www.icpsr.umich.edu/icpsrweb/ICPSR/
Justice Center: Council of State Governments
http://www.justicecenter.csg.org/
National Institutes of Health
http://www.nih.gov
National Institute of Justice
http://www.ojp.usdoj.gov/nij/funding/graduate-research-ellowship/
welcome.htm
National Institute of Mental Health
http://grants.nih.gov/grants/guide/pa-files/PAR-06-217.html
National Institute on Drug Abuse
http://www.nida.nih.gov/researchers.html
Office of Justice Programs
http://www.ojp.usdoj.gov/funding/solicitations.htm
Office of Juvenile Justice and Delinquency Prevention
http://www.ojjdp.gov/
The Sentencing Project
http://www.sentencingproject.org
Social Work and Criminal Justice
http://sw-cj.org
Substance Abuse and Mental Health Services Administration
http://www.samhsa.gov

Appendix 5

Excerpts from an Institutional Review Board Study

Example: Excerpt from a Cross-Sectional Mixed-Methods Study of Social Support of Prisoners and Former Prisoners.

> A.4.1. **Brief Summary.** Provide a *brief* nontechnical description of the study.

Purpose: The overall purpose of the study is to explore the connection to and availability of formal and informal social support to people as they transition from prisons to communities. Aim 1: Describe the referrals to community-based social services that inmates receive immediately prior to release from prison and the characteristics of inmates who receive and who do not receive these referrals. Aim 2: Describe inmates' perceptions of the type of informal social support available to them once they leave prison. Aim 3: Analyze the amount of perceived social support and types of perceived social support for formerly incarcerated persons. Describe the amount of perceived social support and types of perceived social support for this population from the perspective of corrections professionals and formerly incarcerated postreleasees. Aim 4: From the perspective of corrections professionals and formerly incarcerated postre-leasees, what role does social support play in transitional planning?

Participants: Research participants for Aims 1 and 2 include inmates in *XYZ State* prisons as well as information obtained from existing *XYZ State* Department of Correction (DOC) administrative data. Research participants for Aims 3 and 4 include prison-based case manager/social workers, probation officers, and formerly incarcerated postreleasees.

Procedures (methods): Structured interview questions and adminis-trative records will be used to collect data for research Aims 1 and 2. Focus groups and qualitative interviews will be used to collect data for research Aims 3 and 4.

> A.4.2. **Purpose and Rationale.** Provide a summary of the background infor-mation, state the research question(s), and indicate why the study is needed.

Claiming the highest incarceration rate in the world, America's pris-ons house approximately 1.5 million people (Sabol, Couture, & Harrison, 2007) on any given day and nearly 635,000 people are released from state prisons to communities each year (Langan & Levine, 2002). Of the 1700 people released from prisons each day, 68% will be rearrested or reincarcerated within 3 years (Langan & Levine, 2002). Over the past three decades, criminologists outlined effective correctional practice approaches that if followed help to reduce reincarceration rates by reduc-ing criminal reoffending. Accordingly, millions of State and Federal monies are directed toward transitional programs, known as "reentry" programs, that incorporate many of the effective correctional practice principles. Much attention is given to these reentry programs in the criminological literature. However, such reentry programs often have stringent eligibility criteria driven by the program funding source or oth-erwise do not have the capacity to serve all offenders released from pris-ons to communities. The reentry programs, with all their related promise and innovation, have drawn attention away from routine transitional strategies that occur in most correctional facilities and with most people released from prison. The overall purpose of this study is to understand one such aspect of these transitional strategies—the connection of inmates leaving prison to community-based formal social support and informal prosocial support.

The research questions for this study address both formal and informal social support of people as they transition from prisons to communities. Social support in this context refers only to prosocial support—people (or organizations) that help the offender to attain a prosocial (i.e., noncriminal) lifestyle after release. This study will address the following research questions: (1) What are the characteristics of inmates who are referred to community-based services prior to release? To what type of services are they referred? (2) What are inmates' perceptions of the types and amount of informal prosocial support available to them after release from prison? (3) What type and amount of both formal and informal social support do DOC professionals perceive as available to inmates after they are released from prison? What do formerly incarcerated postreleasees perceive? and (4) From the perspective of DOC professionals and postreleasees, what role does social support play in transitional planning? A brief literature review provides the context for this exploratory study and helps to demonstrate the need for a better understanding of the role of social support[1] in prisoner reentry.

The subsequent literature review in this application included a literature-based discussion addressing the following:

- Risk and Protective Factors for Postrelease Reoffense
- Effective Practice in Prisoner Reentry
- Social Support
- Current Correctional Practices and Social Support

A.4.4. **Inclusion/Exclusion Criteria.** List the required characteristics of potential participants, and those that preclude enrollment or involvement of participants or their data. Justify the exclusion of any group, especially by criteria based on gender, ethnicity, race, or age. If pregnant women are excluded, or if women who become pregnant are withdrawn, specific justification must be provided.

For the purposes of each Aim, we will recruit a convenience sample for this exploratory study.

Aims 1 and 2: Structured interview questions and administrative data.

The participant population will be within no more than 45 days of release at the time of study enrollment. The Department of Correction, Division of Prisons (DOP) is a decentralized prison system in which inmates are frequently moved between correctional centers. However, the DOP attempts to move inmates to a correctional center located near the inmate's planned county of release. It is expected that recruitment of inmates who are within 45 days of release will help to reduce study attrition due to the movement of an inmate between correctional centers (i.e., prisons). Inmates must plan to release to *XYZ County*, in *ABC State*. This city was chosen because of the high number of prison releases to this area each month and because of the number of community-based service agencies located in *DEF City*. No persons will be excluded from the study based on ethnicity or race. However, participants must be adults (18 years or older) and participants must be capable of giving informed consent. Participants must be English speaking because the research instruments are in English only and the data collectors speak only English. The participant population is restricted to men. Research indicates social support operates differently for male and female offenders. Given the small sample size, there is a limited ability to address the interaction effects of gender; therefore if both men and women were included in the study the results could be confounded.

In the larger research for which this study serves as a pilot, it will be important to assess whether our preliminary findings describe Spanish-speaking inmates who are not fluent in English, as well as women inmates. However, because we do not have the resources to provide translation of study materials and bilingual interviewers and also to enable us to draw meaningful inferences from this small pilot study, we are seeking a relatively homogeneous group of English-speaking men.

Aims 3 and 4: Focus groups and qualitative interviews.

Prison-based case manager/social workers. The eligible case manager/social workers for the focus groups include all case manager/social workers who have any responsibility to assist inmates in release planning.

The case manager/social workers' participation is strictly voluntary. The DOC will help the Principal Investigator to identify one or two correctional centers in the *DEF* area from which the case manager/social workers will be recruited for study participation. The only exclusionary criteria for this participant population is that the participant has held the current job title for a minimum of 3 months. The minimum job tenure is required to be sure the professional has adequate information and experience to contribute to the focus group.

Probation officers. The eligible probation officers for the focus groups include all probation officers who have any responsibility to supervise postreleasees sentenced to postrelease supervision. The probation officer's participation is strictly voluntary. The DOC will help the Principal Investigator to identify one or two probation units in the *DEF* area from which the probation officers will be recruited for study participation. The only exclusionary criteria for this participant population is that the probation officer must have been in the current job position for a minimum of 3 months. The minimum job tenure is required to be sure the professional has adequate information and experience to contribute to the focus group.

A.4.7. **Full Description of Risks and Measures to Minimize Risks.** Include the risk of psychosocial harm (e.g., emotional distress, embarrassment, breach of confidentiality), economic harm (e.g., loss of employment or insurability, loss of professional standing or reputation, loss of standing within the community), and legal jeopardy (e.g., disclosure of illegal activity or negligence), as well as known side effects of study medication, if applicable, and risk of pain and physical injury. Describe what will be done to minimize these risks. Describe procedures for follow-up, when necessary, such as when participants are found to be in need of medical or psychological referral. If there is no direct interaction with participants, and risk is limited to breach of confidentiality (e.g., for existing data), state this.

Aims 1 and 2: Structured interview questions and administrative data.

Inmate participants will not be exposed to physically harmful risks. Participants may become emotionally distressed when thinking and talking about the following: their forthcoming release plans, the processes associated with planning their transition back to the community, the availability of community-based social services, their referral to community-based services, or the availability of informal (e.g., family, friends, neighbors) social support. Participants may feel embarrassed or ashamed when thinking and talking about the following: their referral to community-based services, their community-based service needs, or the availability of informal social support. In addition, the participant may experience emotional distress or embarrassment if he has difficulty understanding or completing the structured interview questions due to cognitive disabilities, learning disabilities, or learning competence.

To minimize risks to the participants, the potential risks will be disclosed to eligible inmates during the consent process. Participants will be informed that they can refuse to answer or terminate the study at any point during the structured interviews, with no consequence. If a participant is found to be in need of minor medical or psychological referral, the participant will be encouraged to share this information with his prison-based case manager or prison-based social worker. If the medical or psychological need appears to place the participant at risk of harming himself or others, the Principal Investigator will immediately share the medical or psychological risk information with the participant's prison-based case manager/social worker. The consent form will describe this procedure.

Aims 3 and 4: Focus groups and qualitative interviews.

Prison-based case manager/social workers. Case manager/social workers will be identified as eligible to participate in the study by DOC managers. Because the focus groups will be held during work hours, it is likely that DOC managers will know when their personnel are to attend the focus group and thus may be able to deduce whether the professional participated in the study. To minimize the consequences of the managers' knowledge of staff participation, the Principal Investigator will request that managers inform their staff that they are under no obligation to participate in the study and that the staff member will not suffer consequences because of lack of participation. In addition, both the managers and the participants will be reminded that the Principal Investigator will keep confidential individual contributions to the focus group. Although confidentiality can be ensured by the researchers, the researchers cannot ensure that other focus group participants will keep the focus group content confidential. The participants will be informed of this limitation to confidentiality during the consent process.

The case manager/social workers could experience some emotional distress as a result of any of the following: if the case manager/social worker perceives he or she should know more or less about the availability of community-based social service support or informal social support for inmates; if upon hearing other participant responses, the case manager/social worker compares his or her job performance to the job performance of others in the group; and if, despite assurances otherwise, the case manager/social worker is concerned about any elements of his or her participation status being disclosed to supervisors, or if the case manager/social worker believes any information he or she disclosed could threaten his or her reputation among other case manager/social workers.

To minimize risks to the participants, the potential risks will be disclosed to eligible case managers/social workers during the consent process. Participants will be informed that they can refuse to answer or terminate the study at any point during the focus group, with no consequence. In addition, the participants will be told that the Principle Investigator will avoid "round robin" approaches that pressure individuals to speak to certain questions and that no individual will be called on to answer a certain question. Prior to beginning the focus group discussion of the research questions, the researcher will request that the participants respect others rights to confidentiality and discuss the seriousness of a breach in confidentiality.

If a participant seems to be experiencing more than minor distress, information will be provided about support and counseling services, including how to contact the Employee Assistance Program. The Principal Investigator will obtain contact information for support services from DOC R&P prior to conducting the focus group. If a participant seems to be experiencing more than minor distress, the Principal Investigator will suggest the focus group take a break and reconvene in 10 minutes. To avoid further discomfort, the Principal Investigator will ask to speak privately to the participant once the break begins and then provide the participant with support information.

Appendix 6

Excerpt from a Consent Form for a Trial of a Social Support Intervention

University Title
Consent to Participate in a Research Study
Adult Participants: Department of Correction prisoners.

Study and Principal Investigator information provided here.

Excerpts from the Application:

Why are we doing this study?

The goal of the study is to learn about ways to increase support available for people after release from prison. As a part of this study we are trying to find out whether building and strengthening a person's positive social support can help that person to avoid abusing alcohol and to remain drug free and crime free after release from prison.

You are being asked to be in the study because you will be released from prison within the next few weeks and you are returning to *DEF City, ABC State.* We chose people near release to ask them about support they think they will have after prison. We chose *DEF* because of the size of the city.

How long will your part in this study last?

Your part in the study will depend on the group of study participants in which you are enrolled. One group of participants will complete interviews in prison only. Participation in the study for this group will last for 1 to 1½ hours. Participants in the other two groups will be involved in the study while in prison and also while in the community. For members of these two groups, participation in the study will last 1 to 1½ hours while they are in prison. After prison, one of the group's involvement in the study will include three 1- to 2-hour interview sessions over a 6-month period. This same group will talk with a research team member for approximately 10 minutes a week for the first 3 months after prison. The other group will have the same time commitments. In addition, they will meet for a group program for 2 hours a week for 10 weeks.

What will happen if you take part in the study?

If you decide to be in this study, you will do the following things. Remember, you can decide to stop being in the study at any point.

First, review additional information about you that we would like to have from DOC with your consent to participate in this study. We will go over the information that we will request from DOC in a few minutes, before you are asked to decide if you want to be in the study or do not want to be in the study.

Second, sign the consent form. The consent form is the information we are reviewing now.

Third, from interview forms I will read questions to you about the type of social support you had before you came to prison and the type of support you expect to have once you are released from prison. I will write down your responses on the interview form.

Fourth, from other interview forms I will read questions to you about your history of substance use prior to coming from prison.

Fifth, I will ask you if there is a support person in the community that you think would participate in the *Support Matters* program that I described to you earlier. This participation would occur only if you were randomly assigned to that condition. If there is a support person that you think you would like to ask to participate, I will ask you to contact that person and ask if they would be involved. I will also ask for their address and phone number so that I can contact them about being in the study as well.

Sixth, any support person that you identify in the community will be contacted. If they are able to participate in the study you will be randomly assigned either to participate in the *Support Matters* program or not to participate in the program but to still receive information about a program in *DEF City* that may help you. Randomly assigned means that the assignment happens by chance and that nothing about you determined the group assignment.

How will your privacy be protected?

Your name will not be associated with any surveys, only a meaningless code number. That code number will be linked to your prison ID number, but that information will be kept on a list that is stored in a locked file cabinet in the research office at the university and on a password-protected computer. The code number will not be available to anyone but the research team members and the Principal Investigator. Once the study has ended, the Principal Investigator will shred the list of meaningless code numbers and prison ID numbers and delete any electronic record of the list. Participants will not be identified in any report or publication about this study. The staff members of the Department of Correction are not conducting this research project. They will not get a copy of your name or of your answers. The Department will receive a copy of the overall results at the end of the study but will not be able to identify you personally from the copy they receive.

You should know that if you indicate plans to harm yourself, to harm someone else, or to escape, that information will immediately be reported to the appropriate prison officials. After release from prison, plans to harm yourself or to harm someone else will be reported to the local authorities.

Will you receive anything for being in this study?

If you are in the group that is involved in the study after release from prison, you will receive up to a total of $90 for completion of interviews and going to group sessions or completing the weekly interviews with a research team member.

SAMPLE

CONSENT TO ACT AS A PARTICIPANT IN A RESEARCH STUDY
   TITLE: Multidimensional Characteristics of Incarcerated Youth and the Role of Race

   PRINCIPAL INVESTIGATOR:
   CO-INVESTIGATORS:
   SOURCE OF SUPPORT:
   CHILD ADVOCATE:

Why is this study being done?

We want to know about the thoughts, attitudes, and behaviors of youth at residential treatment centers. We want to know about your experiences with school, friends, family, using drugs, drinking, getting in fights, and sexual transmitted diseases (STDs). We want to know what you think of the police, the judges, and the juvenile justice system. We also want to know about different types of services you may have received and other challenges you have faced.

Who is being asked to take part in this study?

About 300 hundred people who are aged 14–18 years and in residential facilities will be invited to be in this study.

What am I being asked to do?

You are being asked to complete an interview that asks questions about past behaviors, drug use, current feelings, and thoughts. If you agree to be in this study, you sign this form. We will interview you in a private room at the [Facility]. The interview is about 60–90 minutes and asks questions about past behaviors, drug use, current feelings, and thoughts. You can look at the questions before you decide if you want to be in the study.

Is my being in this study voluntary?

Yes! Being in this research study is voluntary. You can choose not to provide consent to take part in this research study, even after signing this form. If you decide not to be in the study, this will not affect your treatment or length of stay at [Facility] in any way. You can decide to stop participating at any time. If you decide not to sign the form, then you cannot be in the study.

Are there any costs to be in this study?

No, being in this study will not cost anything. For the time you spend being interviewed, you will get snacks and drinks.

What are the risks to being in this study?

There is little risk involved with this study. The major risk is that you may feel uncomfortable when answering some questions, such as the questions about your feelings or experiences you had. If this happens, then you can talk about it with the interviewers. You do not have to answer a question if you do not want to. Another unlikely risk is you might also be teased because of your participation in the study. If this does happen, you can tell a staff member. [Facility] staff knows about this, and will watch to make sure it does not happen.

Another risk with being in the study is that confidential information about you may be shared by accident. We will do everything possible to protect your privacy. All of us are trained to keep the information about you confidential, and we think the risk of violating confidentiality is small. All records about you being in this study will be kept confidential and will be kept in locked filling cabinets. We remove all identifying information about you from all research documents and your identity will not be revealed in any publication that comes from this study. The confidentiality of all study records will be maintained by following Federal laws.

Will my information be shared with [Facility] staff or anyone else?

No. Your answers will not be shared with staff at [Facility]. The exception to this is if you tell the interviewer that you or someone with whom you are involved is in serious danger or potential harm, we will need to inform the appropriate agencies. If you tell the interviewer that you are going to hurt yourself or others, then this information will be shared with the staff at George Junior Republic.

It is possible that people from the University of Pittsburgh Research Conduct and Compliance Office may review your data for the purpose of monitoring the conduct of this study. In very unusual cases, your research records may be released in response to a court order.

Are there benefits to being in this study?

You will receive no direct benefits from being in the study.

Do I have the right to withdraw from the study?

By signing this form you consent to be in this study. However, you may later change your mind and not let the research team use or share your information. If you decide to do this, the research team may use and share only information already collected for the study. Additionally, your information may still be used and shared if necessary for safety reasons.

Can anyone withdraw me from this study?

You will be withdrawn from the study if we observe a health or mental health problem that does not allow you to finish the interview.

Examples include getting sick, seeing things that other people cannot, having a seizure, or needing medical help.

Who do I call if I have questions or problems?

If you have any questions or concerns about the study, call the investigators listed on the front page of this form. You may also contact [Child Advocate]. [Child Advocate] is serving as the Child Advocate for the project and can help you if you have questions about the study. Any questions you have about your rights as a research subject can be answered by the Human Subjects Protection Advocate at the [IRB Office and Phone #].

VOLUNTARY CONSENT:

The above information has been explained to me and all of my current questions have been answered. I understand that I am encouraged to ask questions about any aspect of this research study during the course of this study, and that such future questions will be answered by a qualified individual or by the investigator(s) listed on the first page of this consent document at the telephone number(s) given. I understand that I may always request that my questions, concerns, or complaints be addressed by a listed investigator.

I understand that I may contact the [IRB and Phone #] to discuss problems, concerns, and questions; obtain information; offer input; or discuss situations that have occurred during my participation.

This research has been explained to me, and I agree to participate.

_____   _____
Subject's Signature   Date

_____
Printed Name of Subject

_____   _____
Signature of Residential Therapeutic Supervisor   Date

CERTIFICATION OF INFORMED CONSENT: I certify that I have explained the nature and purpose of this research study to the above-named individual, and I have discussed the potential benefits and possible risks of study participation. Any questions the individual has about this study have been answered, and we will always be available to address future questions as they arise. I further certify that no research component of this protocol was begun until after this consent form was signed.

_____   _____

Printed Name of Person Obtaining Consent   Role in Research Study

_____   _____

Signature of Person Obtaining Consent   Date

Notes

Preface

[1] This is "defined as social cohesion among neighbors combined with their willingness to intervene on behalf of the common good" (Sampson, Raudenbush, & Earls, 1997, p. 918).

[2] Law enforcement can be considered the doorway into the justice system. Although we do not address research in law enforcement settings in this book, many of the concepts discussed may be directly applied to research with law enforcement agencies. Law enforcement encounters many of the same issues that social workers grapple with and similarly offers important opportunities for research collaboration.

Chapter 4

[1] These definitions were obtained from the U.S. Bureau of Justice Statistics: *http://bjs.ojp.usdoj.gov/index.cfm?ty = tda.*

[2] Refer to the technical appendix for a flow chart of the criminal justice system.

[3] Contact Carrie Pettus-Davis at cpettusdavis@wustl.edu for questions about the *Support Matters* trial.

Appendix 5

[1] Unless otherwise specified, social support will be used to refer to both formal and informal social support throughout the application.

References

Preface

Cuomo, C., Sarachiapone, M., Massimo, D. G., Mancini, M., & Roy, A. (2008). Aggression, impulsivity, personality traits, and childhood trauma of prisoners with substance abuse and addiction. *The American Journal of Drug and Alcohol Abuse, 34,* 339–345.

Dembo, R., & Schmeidler, J. (2003). A classification of high-risk youths. *Crime and Delinquency, 49,* 201–230.

Dembo, R., Schmeidler, J., Nini-gough, B., & Manning, D. (1998). Sociodemographic, delinquency abuse history and psychosocial functioning differences among juvenile offenders of various ages. *Journal of Child and Adolescent Substance Abuse, 8,* 63–78.

Epperson, M., Roberts, L., Tripodi, S., Ivanoff, A., & Gilmer, C. (2009). *The state of criminal justice content in MSW programs in the US.* Paper presented at the Council on Social Work Education, Annual Program Meeting, San Antonio, Texas.

Farrington, D. P., & Welsh, B. (2007). *Saving children from a life of crime.* New York: Oxford University Press.

Glaze, L. E. (2010). *Correctional populations in the United States, 2009.* (NCJ 231681). Washington, DC: Bureau of Justice Statistics.

James, D. J., & Glaze, L. E. (2006). *Mental health problems of prison and jail inmates.* (NCJ 213600). Washington, DC: Bureau of Justice Statistics.

Jang, S. J., & Johnson, B. R. (2001). Neighborhood disorder, individual religiosity, and adolescent use of illicit drugs: A test of multilevel hypotheses. *Criminology, 39,* 109–144.

Krisberg, K., & Howell, J. C. (1998). The impact of the juvenile justice system and prospects for graduated sanctions in a comprehensive strategy. In R. Loeber &

D. P. Farrington (Eds.), *Serious & violent juvenile offenders: Risk factors and successful interventions* (pp. 346–366). Thousand Oaks, CA: Sage Press.

Langan, P. A., & Levin, D. J. (2002). *Recidivism of prisoners released in 1994*. (NCJ 193427). Washington, DC: Bureau of Justice Statistics.

McNulty, T. L., & Bellair, P. E. (2003). Explaining racial and ethnic differences in serious adolescent violent behavior. *Criminology, 41,* 709–748.

Mears, D. P., & Travis, J. (2004). Youth development and reentry. *Youth Violence and Juvenile Justice, 2,* 3–20.

Mumola, C. J., & Karberg, J. C. (2006). *Drug use and dependence state and federal prisoners, 2004.* (NCJ 213530). Washington, DC: Bureau of Justice Statistics.

Petersilia, J. (2003). *When prisoners come home: Parole and prisoner reentry.* New York: Oxford University Press.

Pettus-Davis, C., & Scheyett, A. (2009). *Social work and criminal justice: Are we meeting in the field?* Paper presented at the Council on Social Work Education, Annual Program Meeting, San Antonio, Texas.

Sabol, W. J., West, H. C., & Cooper, M. (2009). *Prisoners in 2008.* (NCJ 228417). Washington, DC: Bureau of Justice Statistics.

Sampson, R. J., Raudenbush, S., & Earls, F. (1997). Neighborhoods and crime: A multilevel study of collective efficacy. *Science, 277,* 918–924.

Sickmund, M. (2004). *Juveniles in corrections.* Washington, DC: Office of Juvenile Justice and Delinquency Prevention.

Chapter 1

Connors, C.K. (1997). *Connors Rating Scales—Revised: Technical manual.* North Tonawanda, NY: Multi-Health Systems.

Grisso, T., & Barnum, R. (2000). *Massachusetts Youth Screening Instrument-2: User's manual and technical report.* Worcester: University of Massachusetts Medical School.

Grisso, T., Barnum, R., Fletcher, K. E., Cauffman, E., & Peuschold, D. (2001). Massachusetts youth screening instrument for mental health needs of juvenile justice youths. *Journal of the American Academy of Child and Adolescent Psychiatry, 40,* 409–418.

Israel, B. A., Schultz, A. J., Parker, E. A., & Becker, A. B. (1998). Review of community-based research: Assessing partnership approaches to improve public health. *Annual Review of Public Health, 19,* 173–202.

Minkler, M. (2005). Community-based research partnerships: Challenges and opportunities. *Journal of Urban Health, 82*(Suppl. 2), 1–12.

OJJDP. (n.d.). Juvenile justice system structure and process. *Statistical Briefing Book.* Office of Juvenile Justice and Delinquency Prevention, U.S. Department of Justice, Office of Justice Programs. Retrieved from http://www.ojjdp.gov/ojstatbb/structure_process/case.html.

Vollmer, T. R., Sloman, K. N., & Samaha, A. L. (2009). Self-injury. In J. L. Matson (Ed.), *Applied behavior analysis for children with autism spectrum disorders* (pp. 157–174). New York: Springer.

Chapter 2

Adler, I., & Kandel, D. B. (1982). A cross-cultural comparison of sociopsychological factors in alcohol use among adolescents in Israel, France, and the United States. *Journal of Youth and Adolescence, 11*, 89–113.

Baker, L. A. (1986). Estimating genetic correlations among discontinuous phenotypes: An analysis of criminal convictions and psychiatric-hospital diagnoses in Danish adoptees. *Behavior Genetics, 16*, 127–142.

Baker, L. A., Mack, W., Moffitt, T., & Mednick, S. (1989). Sex differences in property crime in a Danish adoption cohort. *Behavior Genetics, 19*, 355–370.

Barnes, P. M., Powell-Griner, E., McFann, K., & Nahin R. L. (2004). Complementary and alternative medicine use among adults: United States, 2002. *National Health Statistics Report, 343*, 1–19.

Blanchard, J. M., Vernon, P. A., & Harris, J. A. (1995). A behavior genetic investigation of multiple dimensions of aggression. *Behavior Genetics, 25*, 256.

Bohman, M. (1978). Some genetic aspects of alcoholism and criminality: A population of adoptees. *Archives of General Psychiatry, 35*, 269–276.

Bohman, M., Cloninger, C. R., Sigvardsson, S., & von Knorring, A.-L. (1982). Predisposition to petty criminality in Swedish adoptees: I. Genetic and environment heterogeneity. *Archives of General Psychiatry, 39*, 1233–1241.

Bouchard, T. J., & McGue, M. (1990). Genetic and rearing environmental influences on adult personality: An analysis of adopted twins reared apart. *Journal of Personality, 58*, 263–292.

Brandon, K., & Rose, R. J. (1995). A multivariate twin family study of the genetic and environmental structure of personality, beliefs, and alcohol use [Abstract]. *Behavior Genetics, 25*, 257.

Brunswick, A F., & Messeri, P. (1986). Drugs, lifestyle, and health: A longitudinal study of urban black youth. *American Journal of Public Health, 76*(1), 52–57.

Cadoret, R. J. (1978). Psychopathology in adopted-away offspring of biologic parents with antisocial behavior. *Archives of General Psychiatry, 35*, 176–184.

Cadoret, R. J., Cunningham, L., Loftus, R., & Edwards, J. (1975). Studies of adoptees from psychiatrically disturbed biological parents: II. Temperament, hyperactive, antisocial and developmental variables. *Journal of Pediatrics, 87*, 301–306.

Cadoret, R. J., O'Gorman, T. W., Troughton, E., & Heywood, E. (1985). Alcoholism and antisocial personality: Interrelationships, genetic and environmental factors. *Archives of General Psychiatry, 42*, 161–167.

Cadoret, R. J., & Stewart, M. A. (1991). An adoption study of attention deficit/hyperactivity/aggression and their relationship to adult antisocial personality. *Comprehensive Psychiatry, 32*, 73–82.

Cadoret, R. J., Troughton, E., Bagford, J., & Woodworth, G. (1990). Genetic and environmental factors in adoptee antisocial personality. *European Archives of Psychiatry and Neurological Sciences, 239*, 231–240.

Cadoret, R. J., Troughton, E., & O'Gorman, T. W. (1987). Genetic and environmental factors in alcohol abuse and antisocial personality. *Journal of Studies on Alcohol, 48*, 1–8.

Cadoret, R. J., Troughton, E., O'Gorman, T. W., & Heywood, E. (1986). An adoption study of genetic and environmental factors in drug abuse. *Archives of General Psychiatry, 43*, 1131–1136.

Cairns, R. B., & Cairns, B. D. (1994). *Lifelines and risks, pathways of youth in our time.* Cambridge, England: University of Cambridge Press.

California Department of Corrections & Rehabilitation. (2007). *Juvenile Justice Data Project.* Sacramento, CA: K. Hennigan & K. Kolnick. Retrieved from http://www.cdcr.ca.gov/Reports_Research/docs/JJDP_summary_rpt.pdf.

Capaldi, D. M., and Patterson, G. R. (1996). Can violent offenders be distinguished from frequent offenders? Prediction from childhood to adolescence. *Journal of Research in Crime and Delinquency, 33*, 206–231.

Carey, G. (1992). Twin imitation for antisocial behavior: Implications for genetic and family environment research. *Journal of Abnormal Psychology, 101*, 18–25.

Cates, D. S., Houston, B. K., Vavak, C. R., Crawford, M. H., & Uttley, M. (1993). Heritability of hostility-related emotions, attitudes, and behaviors. *Journal of Behavioral Medicine, 16*, 237–256.

Centers for Disease Control and Prevention. (2005). *Youth Risk Behavior Survey.* Atlanta, GA: CDC.

Centerwall, B. S., & Robinette, C. D. (1989). Twin concordance for dishonorable discharge from the military: With a review of genetics of antisocial behavior. *Comprehensive Psychiatry, 30*, 442–446.

Children's Defense Fund. (2010). *State of America's Children 2010 Report.* Washington, DC.

Christiansen, K. O. (1973). Mobility and crime among twins. *International Journal of Criminology and Penology, 1*, 31–45.

Christiansen, K. O. (1974). Seriousness of criminality and concordance among Danish twins. In R. Hood (Ed.), *Crime, criminology, and public policy* (pp. 63–77). London: Heinemann.

Christiansen, K. O. (1977). A preliminary study of criminality among twins. In S. A. Mednick & K. O. Christiansen (Eds.), *Biological bases of criminal behavior* (pp. 89–108). New York: Gardner Press.

Clear, T. R. (2010). Policy and evidence: The challenge to the American Society of Criminology: 2009 presidential address to the American Society for Criminology. *Criminology, 48*, 1–25.

Cloninger, C. R., Christiansen, K. O., Reich, T., & Gottesman, I. I. (1978). Implications of sex differences in the prevalences of antisocial personality, alcoholism, and criminality for familial transmission. *Archives of General Psychiatry, 35*, 941–951.

Coccaro, E. F., Bergeman, C. S., Kavoussi, R. J., & Seroczynski, A. D. (1997). Heritability of aggression and irritability: A twin study of the Buss–Durkee aggression scales in adult male subjects. *Biological Psychiatry, 41*, 264–272.

Cunningham, L., Cadoret, R. J., Loftus, R., & Edwards, J. E. (1975). Studies of adoptees from psychiatrically disturbed biological parents: Psychiatric conditions in childhood and adolescence. *British Journal of Psychiatry, 126*, 534–549.

Deater-Deckard, K., & Plomin, R. (1999). An adoption study of the etiology of teacher and parent reports of externalizing behavior problems in middle childhood. *Child Development, 70*, 144–154.

Deater-Deckard, K., Reiss, D., Hetherington, E. M., & Plomin, R. (1997). Dimensions and disorders of adolescent adjustment: A quantitative genetic analysis of unselected samples and selected extremes. *Journal of Child Psychology and Psychiatry, 38*, 515–525.

DiLalla, D. L., Carey, G., Gottesman, I. I., & Bouchard, T. J. (1996). Heritability of MMPI personality indicators of psychopathology in twins reared apart. *Journal of Abnormal Psychology, 105*, 491–499.

Earls, F. (2002). Project on human development in Chicago neighborhoods: Longitudinal cohort study, 1994-2001 (HDl:1902.1/01953). Cambridge, MA: Murray Research Archive.

Eaves, L. J., Silberg, J. L., Meyer, J. M., Maes, H. H., Simonoff, E., Pickles, A., et al. (1997). Genetics and developmental psychopathology: II. The main effects of genes and environment on behavioral problems in the Virginia Twin Study of Adolescent Behavioral Development. *Journal of Child Psychology and Psychiatry and Allied Disciplines, 38*, 965–980.

Eley, T. C., Lichtenstein, P., & Stevenson, J. (1999). Sex differences in the etiology of aggressive and nonaggressive antisocial behavior: Results from two twin studies. *Child Development, 70*, 155–168.

Elliot, D. S. (1994). Serious violent offenders: Onset, developmental course, and termination. *Criminology, 32*, 1–21.

Elliot, P. (2007). Three Generations Combined, 1965–1997: Inter-university Consortium for Political and Social Research (ICPSR) [distributor].

Elliott, D. (2009). National Youth Survey [United States]: Wave VII, 1987: Inter-university Consortium for Political and Social Research (ICPSR) [distributor].

Eron, L. D., & Huesmann, L. R. (1990). The stability of aggressive behavior–even onto the third generation. In M. Lewis & S. M. Miller (Eds.), *Handbook of developmental psychopathology* (pp. 147–156). New York: Plenum.

Farrington, D. P. (2003). Key results from the first 40 years of the Cambridge Study in Delinquent Development. In T. P. Thornberry & M. D. Krohn (Eds.), *Taking stock of delinquency: An overview of findings from contemporary longitudinal studies*. New York: Kluwer/Plenum.

Ferdinand, R. F., & Verhulst, F. C. (1994). The prediction of poor outcome in young adults: Comparison of the Young Adult Self-Report, the General Health Questionnaire and the Symptom Checklist. *Acta Psychiatrica Scandinavica, 89,* 405–410.

Ferguson, D. M., Hopwood, L. J., & Lynskey, M. (1994). The childhoods of multiple problem adolescents: A 15 year longitudinal study. *Journal of Child Psychology and Psychiatry, 35,* 1123–1140.

Fienberg, S. E. (1994). Sharing statistical data in the biomedical and health sciences: Ethical, institutional, legal, and professional dimensions. *Annual Review of Public Health, 15,* 1–18.

Finkel, D., & McGue, M. (1997). Sex differences and nonadditivity in heritability of the multidimensional personality questionnaire scales. *Journal of Personality and Social Psychology, 72,* 929–938.

Gabrielli, W. F., & Mednick, S. A. (1984). Urban environment, genetics, and crime. *Criminology, 22,* 645–652.

Ghodsian-Carpey, J., & Baker, L. A. (1987). Genetic and environmental influences on aggression in 4- to 7-year-old twins. *Aggressive Behavior, 13,* 173–186.

Glueck, S., & Glueck, E. (1968). *Delinquents and non-delinquents in perspective.* Cambridge, MA: Harvard University Press.

Gottesman, I. I. (1965). Personality and natural selection. In S. G. Vandenberg (Ed.), *Methods and goals in human behavior genetics* (pp. 63–80). New York: Academic Press.

Gottesman, I. I. (1966). Genetic variance in adaptive personality traits. *Journal of Child Psychology and Psychiatry, 7,* 199–208.

Gottesman, I. I., Carey, G., & Bouchard, T. J. (1984, May). *The Minnesota Multiphasic Personality Inventory of identical twins raised apart.* Paper presented at the meeting of the Behavior Genetics Association, Bloomington, IN.

Grove, W. M., Eckert, E. D., Heston, L., Bouchard, T. J., Segal, N., & Lykken, D. T. (1990). Heritability of substance abuse and antisocial behavior: A study of monozygotic twins reared apart. *Biological Psychiatry, 27,* 1293–1304.

Gustavsson, J. P., Pedersen, N. L., Åsberg, M., & Schalling, D. (1996). Exploration into the sources of individual differences in aggression-, hostility-, and anger-related (AHA) personality traits. *Personality and Individual Differences, 21,* 1067–1071.

Haapanen, R., & Steiner, H. (2006). Assessing mental health problems among serious delinquents committed to the California Youth Authority, 1997–1999 [Computer file]. ICPSR04337-v1. Sacramento, CA: California Youth Authority, 1999.

Hancock, G. R., & Miller, R. O. (2010). *The reviewer's guide to quantitative methods in the social sciences.* New York: Routledge Press.

Harris, K. M., & Udry, J. R. (2011). National Longitudinal Study of Adolescent Health (Add Health), 1990–2008: Political Context Database [Restricted Use]: Inter-university Consortium for Political and Social Research (ICPSR) [distributor].

Hershberger, S. L., Billig, J. P., Iacono, W. G., & McGue, M. (1995). Life events, personality, and psychopathology in late adolescence: Genetic and environmental factors [Abstract]. *Behavior Genetics, 25,* 270.

Horn, J. M., Plomin, R., & Rosenman, R. (1976). Heritability of personality traits in adult male twins. *Behavior Genetics, 6,* 17–30.

Howard, M. O., & Vaughn, M. G. (2008). Disseminating results and sharing data and publications. In A. R. Stiffman (Ed.), *The field research survival guide* (pp. 233–256). Oxford, UK: Oxford University Press.

Huizinga, D. (1995). Developmental sequences in delinquency: Dynamic typologies. In L.J. Crockett & A.C. Crouter (Eds.), *Pathways through adolescence* (pp. 15–34). Hillsdale, NJ: Lawrence Erlbaum.

Hunt, D., & Rhodes, W. (2011). Arrestee Drug Abuse Monitoring Program II in the United States, 2010: Inter-university Consortium for Political and Social Research (ICPSR) [distributor].

Hutchings, B., & Mednick, S. A. (1971). Criminality in adoptees and their adoptive and biological parents: A pilot study. In S. A. Mednick & K. O. Christiansen (Eds.), *Biosocial bases of criminal behavior* (pp. 127–141). New York: Gardner Press.

Jessor, R., Donovan, J. E., & Costa, F. M. (1991). *Beyond adolescence: Problem behavior and young adult development.* New York: Cambridge University Press.

Johnson, J. G., Smailes, E., Cohen, P., Kasen, S., and Brook, J. S. (2004). Antisocial parental behavior, problematic parenting, and aggressive offspring behavior during adulthood. *British Journal of Criminology, 44,* 915–930.

Johnston, L. D., Bachman, J. G., O'Malley, P. M., & Schulenberg, J. E. (2010). Monitoring the Future: A Continuing Study of American Youth (12th-Grade Survey), 2009: Inter-university Consortium for Political and Social Research (ICPSR) [distributor].

Kolvin, I., Miller, F. J. W., Fleeting, M., & Kolvin, P. A. (1988). Social and parenting factors affecting criminal-offense rates: Findings from the Newcastle Thousand Family Study (1947–1980). *British Journal of Psychiatry, 152,* 80–90.

Lattimore, P. K., Linster, R., MacDonald, J., Visher, C., & Piquero, A. (2004). Studying frequency of arrest among high and low rate of offenders. *Journal of Research in Crime and Delinquency, 41,* 37–57.

LeBlanc, M. (1996). Changing patterns in the perpetration of offenses over time: Trajectories from early adolescence to the early thirties. *Studies on Crime and Crime Prevention, 5,* 151–165.

Livesley, W. J., Jang, K. L., Jackson, D. N., & Vernon, P. A. (1993). Genetic and environmental contributions to dimensions of personality disorder. *American Journal of Psychiatry, 150,* 1826–1831.

Loeber, R., Green, S. M., Keenan, K., & Lahey, B. B. (1995). Which boys will fare worse? Early predictors of the onset of conduct disorder in a six-year longitudinal study. *Journal of the American Academy of Child and Adolescent Psychiatry, 34,* 499–509.

Loehlin, J. C., & Nichols, R. C. (1976). *Heredity, environment, and personality.* Austin: University of Texas Press.

Loehlin, J. C., Willerman, L., & Horn, J. M. (1985). Personality resemblance in adoptive families when the children are late-adolescent or adult. *Journal of Personality and Social Psychology, 48,* 376–392.

Loehlin, J. C., Willerman, L., & Horn, J. M. (1987). Personality resemblance in adoptive families: A 10-year follow-up. *Journal of Personality and Social Psychology, 53,* 961–969.

Lykken, D. T., Tellegen, A., & DeRubeis, R. (1978). Volunteer bias in twin research: The rule of two-thirds. *Social Biology, 25,* 1–9.

Lyons, M. J., True, W. R., Eisen, S. A., Goldberg, J., Meyer, J. M., Faraone, S. V., et al. (1995). Differential heritability of adult and juvenile antisocial traits. *Archives of General Psychiatry, 52,* 906–915.

Lytton, H., Watts, D., & Dunn, B. E. (1988). Stability of genetic determination from age 2 to age 9: A longitudinal twin study. *Social Biology, 35,* 62–73.

MacArthur Research Foundation Network on Adolescent Development and Juvenile Justice. (2002). *Adolescents' Competence to Stand Trial–MacArthur Juvenile Competence Study.* Philadelphia, PA: Temple University, Department of Psychology, MacArthur Foundation Research Network on Adolescent Development and Juvenile Justice. Retrieved from http://www.adjj.org/content/page.php?cat_id=2&content_id=8.

McCord, J. (1991). Family relationships, juvenile delinquency, and adult criminality. *Criminology, 29,* 397–417.

McCord, J., & Ensminger, M. E. (1997). Multiple risks and comorbidity in an African-American population. *Criminal Behavior and Mental Health, 7,* 339–352.

McGue, M., Bacon, S., & Lykken, D. T. (1993). Personality stability and change in early adulthood: A behavioral genetic analysis. *Developmental Psychology, 29,* 96–109.

McGue, M., Sharma, A., & Benson, P. (1996). The effect of common rearing on adolescent adjustment: Evidence from a U.S. adoption cohort. *Developmental Psychology, 32,* 604–613.

Mednick, S. A., Gabrielli, W. F., & Hutchings, B. (1983). Genetic influences in criminal behavior: Evidence from an adoption cohort. In K. T. Van Dusen & S. A. Mednick (Eds.), *Prospective studies of crime* and delinquency (pp. 39–56). Boston: Kluwer-Nijhoff.

Meininger, J. C., Hayman, L. L., Coates, P. M., & Gallagher, P. (1988). Genetics or environment? Type A behavior and cardiovascular risk factors in twin children. *Nursing Research, 37,* 341–346.

Moffit, T. E., Caspi, A., Rutter, M., and Silva, P. A. (2001). *Sex differences in antisocial behavior.* Cambridge: Cambridge University Press.

Nathawat, S. S., & Puri, P. (1995). A comparative study of MZ and DZ twins on Level I and Level II mental abilities and personality. *Journal of the Indian Academy of Applied Psychology, 21,* 87–92.

National Center for Juvenile Justice. (2005). Juvenile Court Statistics, 1997: [United States]: Inter-university Consortium for Political and Social Research (ICPSR) [distributor].

National Center for State Courts. (2007). State Court Statistics, 2004: [United States]: Inter-university Consortium for Political and Social Research (ICPSR) [distributor].

Neiderhiser, J. M., Pike, A., Hetherington, E. M., & Reiss, D. (1998). Adolescent perceptions as mediators of parenting: Genetic and environmental contributions. *Developmental Psychology, 34,* 1459–1469.

O'Connor, M., Foch, T., Sherry, T., & Plomin, R. (1980). A twin study of specific behavior problems of socialization as viewed by parents. *Journal of Abnormal Child Psychology, 8,* 189–199.

O'Connor, T. G., McGuire, S., Reiss, D., Hetherington, E. M., & Plomin, R. (1998). Co-occurrence of depressive symptoms and antisocial behavior in adolescence: A common genetic liability. *Journal of Abnormal Psychology, 107,* 27–37.

O'Connor, T. G., Neiderhiser, J. M., Reiss, D., Hetherington, E. M., & Plomin, R. (1998). Genetic contributions to continuity, change, and co-occurrence of antisocial and depressive symptoms in adolescence. *Journal of Child Psychology and Psychiatry, 39,* 323–336.

Office of Juvenile Justice and Delinquency Prevention. (1999). Report to Congress on Juvenile Violence Research. Washington, DC: U.S. Department of Justice, Office of Justice Programs, Office of Juvenile Justice and Delinquency Prevention. Retrieved from https://www.ncjrs.gov/pdffiles1/176976.pdf.

Office of Juvenile Justice and Delinquency Prevention. (2010). National Juvenile Court Data Archive. Retrieved from http://www.ojjdp.gov/ojstatbb/njcda/.

Ohio State University. Center for Human Resource Research. (2007). National Longitudinal Survey of Mature Women, 1967–2003: Inter-university Consortium for Political and Social Research (ICPSR) [distributor].

Ohio State University. Center for Human Resource Research. (2007). National Longitudinal Survey of Older Men, 1966–1990: Inter-university Consortium for Political and Social Research (ICPSR) [distributor].

Ohio State University. Center for Human Resource Research. (2007). National Longitudinal Survey of Young Men, 1966–1981: Inter-university Consortium for Political and Social Research (ICPSR) [distributor].

Ohio State University. Center for Human Resource Research. (2007). National Longitudinal Survey of Young Women, 1968–2003: Inter-university Consortium for Political and Social Research (ICPSR) [distributor].

Ohio State University. Center for Human Resource Research. (2007). National Longitudinal Survey of Youth, 1997: Inter-university Consortium for Political and Social Research (ICPSR) [distributor].

Owen, D., & Sines, J. O. (1970). Heritability of personality in children. *Behavior Genetics, 1,* 235–248.

Pandina, R. J., Labouvie, E. W., and White, H. R. (1984). Potential contributions of the life span developmental approach to the study of adolescent alcohol and drug use: The Rutgers Health and Human Development Project. *Journal of Drug Issues, 14,* 253–268.

Parker, T. (1989). *Television viewing and aggression in four and seven year old children.* Paper presented at Summer Minority Access to Research Training meeting, University of Colorado, Boulder.

Petersilia, J. R. (1991). *Policy relevance and the future of criminology.* Santa Monica, CA: Rand Corporation.

Pike, A., McGuire, S., Hetherington, E. M., Reiss, D., & Plomin, R. (1996). Family environment and adolescent depressive symptoms and antisocial behavior: A multivariate genetic analysis. *Developmental Psychology, 32,* 590–603.

Plomin, R., & Foch, T. T. (1980). A twin study of objectively assessed personality in childhood. *Journal of Personality and Social Psychology, 39,* 680–688.

Plomin, R., Foch, T. T., & Rowe, D. C. (1981). Bobo clown aggression in childhood: Environment, not genes. *Journal of Research in Personality, 15,* 331–342.

Pogue-Geile, M. F., & Rose, R. J. (1985). Developmental genetic studies of adult personality. *Developmental Psychology, 21,* 547–557.

Pulkkinen, L., & Pitkanen, T. (1993). Continuities in aggressive behavior from childhood to adulthood. *Aggressive Behavior, 19,* 249–223.

Rahe, R. H., Hervig, L., & Rosenman, R. H. (1978). Heritability of Type A behavior. *Psychosomatic Medicine, 40,* 478–486.

Rhee, S. H., & Waldman, I. D. (2002). Genetic and environmental influences on antisocial behavior: A meta-analysis of twin and adoption studies. *Psychological Bulletin, 128*(3), 490–529.

Robins, L. N. (1979). Study childhood predictors of adult outcomes: Replications from longitudinal studies. In J. E. Barrett, R. M. Rose, & A. L. Kleman (Eds.), *Stress and mental disorder* (pp. 219–235). New York: Raven Press.

Rose, R. J. (1988). Genetic and environmental variance in content dimensions of the MMPI. *Journal of Personality and Social Psychology, 55,* 302–311.

Rowe, D. C. (1983). Biometrical genetic models of self-reported delinquent behavior: A twin study. *Behavior Genetics, 13,* 473–489.

Rushton, J. P. (1996). Self-report delinquency and violence in adult twins. *Psychiatric Genetics, 6,* 87–89.

Rushton, J. P., Fulker, D. W., Neale, M. C., Nias, D. K. B., & Eysenck, H. J. (1986). Altruism and aggression: The heritability of individual differences. *Journal of Personality and Social Psychology, 50,* 1192–1198.

Rutter, M. (1981). Epidemiological-longitudinal strategies and causal research in child psychiatry. *Journal of the American Academy of Child Psychiatry, 20,* 513–544.

Scarr, S. (1966). Genetic factors in activity motivation. *Child Development, 37,* 663–673.

Schmitz, S., Cherny, S. S., Fulker, D. W., & Mrazek, D. A. (1994). Genetic and environmental influences on early childhood behavior. *Behavior Genetics, 24,* 25–34.

Schmitz, S., Fulker, D. W., & Mrazek, D. A. (1995). Problem behavior in early and middle childhood: An initial behavior genetic analysis. *Journal of Child Psychology and Psychiatry, 36,* 1443–1458.

Seelig, K. J., & Brandon, K. O. (1997, July). *Rater differences in gene–environment contributions to adolescent problem behavior.* Paper presented at the meeting of the Behavior Genetics Association, Toronto, Ontario, Canada.

Sigvardsson, S., Cloninger, C. R., Bohman, M., & von Knorring, A. L. (1982). Predisposition to petty criminality in Swedish adoptees: III. Sex differences and validation of the male typology. *Archives of General Psychiatry, 39,* 1248–1253.

Silberg, J. L., Erickson, M. T., Meyer, J. M., Eaves, L. M., Rutter, M. L., & Hewitt, J. K. (1994). The application of structural equation modeling to maternal ratings of twins' behavioral and emotional problems. *Journal of Consulting and Clinical Psychology, 62,* 510–521.

Silberg, J., Rutter, M., Meyer, J., Maes, H., Hewitt, J., Simonoff, E., et al. (1996). Genetic and environmental influences on the covariation between hyperactivity and conduct disturbance in juvenile twins. *Journal of Child Psychology and Psychiatry, 37,* 803–816.

Simonoff, E., Pickles, A., Hewitt, J., Silberg, J., Rutter, M., Loeber, L., et al. (1995). Multiple raters of disruptive child behavior: Using a genetic strategy to examine shared views and bias. *Behavior Genetics, 25,* 311–326.

Slutske, W. S., Heath, A. C., Dinwiddie, S. H., Madden, P. A. F., Bucholz, K. K., Dunne, M. P., et al. (1997). Modeling genetic and environmental influences in the etiology of conduct disorder: A study of 2,682 adult twin pairs. *Journal of Abnormal Psychology, 106,* 266–279.

Stevenson, J., & Graham, P. (1988). Behavioral deviance in 13-year-old twins: An item analysis. *Journal of the American Academy of Child and Adolescent Psychiatry, 27,* 791–797.

Taylor, J., McGue, M., Iacono, W. G., & Lykken, D. T. (2000). A behavioral genetic analysis of the relationship between the Socialization scale and self-reported delinquency. *Journal of Personality, 68,* 29–50.

Tellegen, A., Lykken, D. T., Bouchard, T. J., Wilcox, K., Segal, N., & Rich, S. (1988). Personality similarity in twins reared apart and together. *Journal of Personality and Social Psychology, 54,* 1031–1039.

Thornberry, T. P., Krohn, M. D., Lizotte, A. J., Smith, C. A., & Tobin, K. (2003). *Gangs and delinquency in developmental perspective.* New York: Cambridge University Press.

Torgersen, S., Skre, I., Onstad, S., Edvardsen, J., & Kringlen, E. (1993). The psychometric–genetic structure of *DSM–III–R* personality disorder criteria. *Journal of Personality Disorders, 7,* 196–213.

Tremblay, R. E., Masse, B., Perron, D., Le Blanc, M., Schartzman, A. E., & Ledingham, J. E. (1992). Early disruptive behavior, poor school achievement, delinquent behavior. *Journal of Consulting and Clinical Psycholgy, 60,* 64–72.

Tremblay, R. E., Vitaro, F., Nagin, D. S., Pagani, L., & Séguin, J. R. (2003). The Montreal longitudinal and experimental study. In T. P. Thornberry & M. D. Krohn (Eds.0, *Taking stock of delinquency: An overview of findings from contemporary longitudinal studies.* New York: Kluwer/Plenum.

United States Department of Health and Human Services. Centers for Disease Control and Prevention. National Center for Health Statistics. (2011). National Health and Nutrition Examination Survey (NHANES), 2007–2008: Inter-university Consortium for Political and Social Research (ICPSR) [distributor].

United States Department of Health and Human Services. Substance Abuse and Mental Health Services Administration. Office of Applied Studies. (2010). National Survey on Drug Use and Health, 2009: Inter-university Consortium for Political and Social Research (ICPSR) [distributor].

United States Department of Justice. Federal Bureau of Investigation. (2011). Uniform Crime Reporting Program Data: Hate Crime Data, 2009 [Record-Type Files]: Inter-university Consortium for Political and Social Research (ICPSR) [distributor].

United States Department of Justice. Federal Bureau of Investigation. (2011). Uniform Crime Reporting Program Data: Offenses Known and Clearances by Arrest, 2009: Inter-university Consortium for Political and Social Research (ICPSR) [distributor].

United States Department of Justice. Office of Justice Programs. Bureau of Justice Statistics. (2010). Census of Jail Facilities, 2006: Inter-university Consortium for Political and Social Research (ICPSR) [distributor].

United States Department of Justice. Office of Justice Programs. Bureau of Justice Statistics. (2010). Census of State and Federal Adult Correctional Facilities, 2005: Inter-university Consortium for Political and Social Research (ICPSR) [distributor].

United States Department of Justice. Office of Justice Programs. Bureau of Justice Statistics. (2011). Annual Survey of Jails in Indian Country, 2009: Inter-university Consortium for Political and Social Research (ICPSR) [distributor].

United States Department of Justice. Office of Justice Programs. Bureau of Justice Statistics. (2011). Annual Survey of Jails: Jail-Level Data, 2009: Inter-university Consortium for Political and Social Research (ICPSR) [distributor].

United States Department of Justice. Office of Justice Programs. Bureau of Justice Statistics. (2011). National Crime Victimization Survey, 2010: Inter-university Consortium for Political and Social Research (ICPSR) [distributor].

United States Department of Justice. Office of Justice Programs. Office of Juvenile Justice and Delinquency Prevention. (2011). Census of Public and Private Juvenile Detention, Correctional, and Shelter Facilities, 1994–1995: [United States]: Inter-university Consortium for Political and Social Research (ICPSR) [distributor].

van den Oord, E. J. C. G., Boomsma, D. I., & Verhulst, F. C. (1994). A study of problem behaviors in 10- to 15-year-old biologically related and unrelated international adoptees. *Behavior Genetics, 24,* 193–205.

van den Oord, E. J. C. G., Verhulst, F. C., & Boomsma, D. I. (1996). A genetic study of maternal and paternal ratings of problem behaviors in 3-year-old twins. *Journal of Abnormal Psychology, 105,* 349–357.

Wadsworth, M. E. J. (1979). *Roots of delinquency: Infancy, adolescence, and crime.* London: Martin Robertson.

Waldman, I. D., Levy, F., & Hay, D. A. (1995). Multivariate genetic analyses of the overlap among *DSM–III–R* disruptive behavior disorder symptoms. *Behavior Genetics, 25,* 293–294.

Welsh, B., & Farrington, D. P. (2007). *Evidence-based crime prevention.* New York: Routledge Press.

Werner, E. E., & Smith, R. S. (2001). *Journeys from childhood to midlife.* Ithaca, NY: Cornell University Press.

Wikström, P-O. H. (1990). Age and crime in a Stockholm cohort. *Journal of Quantitative Criminology, 6,* 61–84.

Willcutt, E. G., Shyu, V., Green, P., & Pennington, B. F. (1995, April). *A twin study of the comorbidity of the disruptive behavior disorders of childhood.* Paper presented at the annual meeting of the Society for Research in Child Development, Indianapolis, IN.

Wilson, G. D., Rust, J., & Kasriel, J. (1977). Genetic and family origins of humor preferences: A twin study. *Psychological Reports, 41,* 659–660.

World Health Organization. (2002). *Health Behavior in School-Aged Children, 1997–1998: United States.* ICPSR version. Calverton, MD: Macro International, 2002. Ann Arbor, MI: Inter-university Consortium for Political and Sodal Research, 2003.

Young, S. E., Stallings, M. C., Corley, R. P., Hewitt, J. K., & Fulker, D. W. (1996, June). *Parent–offspring transmission of substance use, antisocial behavior, and cognitive factors in selected, adoptive, and control families.* Paper presented at the meeting of the Behavior Genetics Association, Pittsburgh, PA.

Young, S. E., Stallings, M. C., Corley, R. P., Hewitt, J. K., & Fulker, D. W. (1997, July). *Sibling resemblance for conduct disorder and attention deficit-hyperactivity disorder in selected, adoptive, and control families.* Paper presented at the meeting of the Behavior Genetics Association, Toronto, Ontario, Canada.

Zahn-Waxler, C., Schmitz, S., Fulker, D., Robinson, J., & Emde, R. (1996). Behavior problems in 5-year-old monozygotic and dizygotic twins: Genetic and environmental influences, patterns of regulation, and internalization of control. *Development and Psychopathology, 8,* 103–122.

Chapter 3

Armstrong, G. S., & Rodriguez, N. (2005). Effects of individual and contextual characteristics on preadjudication detention of juvenile delinquents. *Justice Quarterly, 22,* 521–539.

Bishop, D. M., & Frazier, C. E. (1996). Race effects in juvenile justice decision-making: Findings of a statewide analysis. *Journal of Criminal Law & Criminology, 86*, 392–414.

Bishop, D. M., Frazier, C. E., Lanza-Kaduce, L., & Winner, L. (1996). The transfer of juveniles to criminal court: Does it make a difference? *Crime & Delinquency, 42*, 171–191.

Fagan, J. (1996). The comparative advantage of juvenile versus criminal court sanctions on recidivism among adolescent felony offenders. *Law and Policy, 18*, 77–114.

Fagan, J., et al. (2003). *Be Careful What You Wish For: The Comparative Impacts of Juvenile versus Criminal Court Sanctions on Recidivism among Adolescent Felony Offenders.* Columbia Law School Public Law & Legal Theory Working Paper Group Paper Number 03-61, New York (http://ssrn.com/abstract = 491202).

Fagan, J., & Deschenes, E. P. (1990). Determinants of judicial waiver decisions for violent juvenile offenders. *Journal of Criminal Law and Criminology, 81*, 314–347.

Fagan, J., Forst, M., & Vivona, S. (1987). Racial determinants of the judicial transfer decision: Prosecuting violent youth in criminal court. *Crime and Delinquency, 33*, 259–286.

Feld, B. C. (1991). Justice by geography: Urban, suburban, and rural variations in juvenile justice administration. *Journal of Criminal Law and Criminology, 82*, 156–210.

Feld, B. C. (1993). *Justice for children: The right to counsel and the juvenile courts.* Boston: Northeastern University Press.

Jonson-Reid, M. (2002). Exploring the relationship between child welfare intervention and juvenile corrections involvement. *American Journal of Orthopsychiatry, 72*, 559–576.

Jonson-Reid, M., & Barth, R. P. (2000a). From maltreatment report to juvenile incarceration: The role of child welfare services. *Child Abuse & Neglect, 24*, 505–520.

Jonson-Reid, M., & Barth, R. P. (2000b). From placement to prison: The path to adolescent incarceration from child welfare supervised foster or group care. *Children and Youth Services Review, 22*, 493–516.

Myers, D. L. (2003). The recidivism of violent youths in juvenile and adult court: A consideration of selection bias. *Youth Violence and Juvenile Justice, 1*, 79–101.

Podkopacz, M. R., & Feld, B. C. (1996). The end of the line: An empirical study of judicial waiver. *Journal of Criminal Law and Criminology, 86*, 449–492.

Podkopacz, M. R., & Feld, B. C. (2001). The back-door to prison: Waiver reform, "blended sentencing," and the law of unintended consequences. *The Journal of Criminal Law and Criminology, 91*(4), 997–1071.

Rodriguez, N. (2007). Juvenile court context and detention decisions: Reconsidering the role of race, ethnicity, and community characteristics in juvenile court processes. *Justice Quarterly, 24,* 629–656.

Ryan, J. P., Herz, D., Hernandez, P. M., & Marshall, J. M. (2007). Maltreatment and delinquency: Investigating child welfare bias in juvenile justice processing. *Children and Youth Services Review, 29,* 1035–1050.

Shook, J. J. (2011). Prosecutorial decisions to treat juveniles as adults: Intersections of individual and contextual characteristics. *The Criminal Law Bulletin, 43,* 341–387.

Shook, J. J., & Goodkind, S. (2009). Racial disproportionality in juvenile justice: The interaction of race and geography in pretrial detention for violent and serious offenders. *Race and Social Problems, 1,* 257–266.

Singer, S. I. (1993). The automatic waiver of juveniles and substantive justice. *Crime and Delinquency, 39,* 253.

Singer, S. I. (1996). *Recriminalizing delinquency: Violent juvenile crime and juvenile justice reform.* Cambridge: Cambridge University Press.

Sridharan, S., Greenfield, G., & Blakley, B. (2004). A study of prosecutorial certification practice in Virginia. *Criminology and Public Policy, 3,* 605.

Wordes, M., Bynum, T. S., & Corley, C. J. (1994). Locking up youth: The impact of race on detention decision. *Journal of Research in Crime and Delinquency, 31,* 149–165.

Chapter 4

Bureau of Justice Statistics. (2011). *All terms and definitions.* Washington, DC: Office of Justice Programs. *http://bjs.ojp.usdoj.gov/index.cfm?ty = tda.*

Campbell, M., French, S., & Gendreau, P. (2009). The prediction of violence of adult offenders: A meta-analytic comparison of instruments and methods of assessment. *Criminal Justice and Behavior, 36,* 567–590.

Hanson, R. K., & Morton-Bourgon, K. E. (2009). The accuracy of recidivism risk assessment for sexual offenders: A meta-analysis of 118 prediction studies. *Psychological Assessment, 21,* 1–21.

Kleck, G., Tark, J., & Bellows, J. J. (2006). What methods are most frequently used in research in criminology and criminal justice? *Journal of Criminal Justice, 34,* 147–152.

National Criminal Justice Reference Service. (2011). *In the spotlight.* Washington, DC: U.S. Department of Justice. http://www.ncjrs.gov/spotlight/drug_courts/Summary.html.

Taxman, S., & Friedman, P. D. (2009). Fidelity and adherence at the transition point: Theoretically driven experiments. *Journal of Experimental Criminology, 5,* 219–226.

Walters, G. D. (2006). Risk-appraisal versus self-report in the prediction of criminal justice outcomes: A meta-analysis. *Criminal Justice and Behavior, 33*, 279–304.

Chapter 5

Cohen, A. S., Kim, S., & Baker, F. B. (1993). Detection of differential item functioning in the graded response model. *Applied Psychological Measurement, 17*, 335–350.

Grant, B. F., Hasin, D. S., Chou, S. P., Stinson, F. S., & Dawson, D. A. (2004). Nicotine dependence and psychiatric disorders in the United States: results from the national epidemiologic survey on alcohol and related conditions. *Archives of General Psychiatry, 61*, 1107–1115.

Grant B. F., Moore, T. C., & Kaplan, K. (2003). *Source and Accuracy Statement: Wave 1 National Epidemiologic Survey on Alcohol and Related Conditions (NESARC)*. Bethesda, MD: National Institute on Alcohol Abuse and Alcoholism.

Grant, B. F., Stinson, F. S., Dawson, D. A., Chou, S. P., Dufour, M. C., Compton, W., Pickering. R. P., & Kaplan K. (2004). Prevalence and co-occurrence of substance use disorders and independent mood and anxiety disorders: Results from the National Epidemiologic Survey on Alcohol and Related Conditions. *Archives of General Psychiatry, 61*, 807–816.

Greenberg, D. F. (2010). Longitudinal criminology. *Journal of Quantitative Criminology, 26*, 437–443.

Hindelang, M. J., Hirschi, T., & Weis, J. G. (1981). *Measuring delinquency*. Beverly Hills, CA: Sage Press.

Howard, M. O., & Vaughn, M. G. (2008). Disseminating results and sharing data and publications. In A. R. Stiffman (Ed.), *The field research survival guide*. Oxford, UK: Oxford University Press.

Thornberry, T. P., & Krohn, M. D. (2003). Comparison of self-report and official data for measuring crime. In J. V. Pepper & C. V. Petrie (Eds.), *Measurement problems in criminal justice research: Workshop summary* (pp. 43–94). Washington, DC: National Academies Press.

Vaughn, M. G., Fu, J., DeLisi, M., Beaver, K. M., Perron, B. E., & Howard, M. O. (2010). Criminal victimization and comorbid substance use and psychiatric disorders in the United States: Results from the NESARC. *Annals of Epidemiology, 20*, 281–288.

Vaughn, M. G., Fu, Q., DeLisi, M., Beaver, K. M., Terrell, K., Perron, B. E., & Howard, M. O. (2009). Correlates of cruelty to animals in the United States: Results from the national epidemiologic survey on alcohol and related conditions. *Journal of Psychiatric Research, 43*, 1213–1218.

Chapter 6

Harris, C., Steffensmeier, D., Ulmer, J. T., & Painter-Davis, N. (2009). Are blacks and hispanics disproportionately incarcerated relative to their arrests?: Racial and ethnic disproportionality between arrest and incarceration. *Race and Social Problems, 1*(4), 187–199.

Kramer, J. H., & Ulmer, J. T. (1996). Sentencing disparity and guidelines departures. *Justice Quarterly, 13*(1), 401–426.

Kramer, J., & Ulmer, J. T. (2002). Downward departures for serious violent offenders: Local court "corrections" to Pennsylvania's sentencing guidelines. *Criminology, 40*(4), 601–636.

Kurlychek, M. C., & Johnson, B. D. (2004). The juvenile penalty: A comparison of juvenile and young adult sentencing outcomes in criminal court. *Criminology, 42*(2), 485–517.

Steffensmeier, D. J., Kramer, J. H., & Ulmer, J. T. (1996). Age differences in sentencing. *Justice Quarterly, 12*(3), 701–719.

Steffensmeier, D. J., Ulmer, J. T., & Kramer, J. H. (1998). The interaction of race, gender, and age in criminal sentencing: The punishment costs of being young, black, and male. *Criminology, 36*(4), 763–797.

Ulmer, J. T., & Kramer, J. H. (1996). Court communities under sentencing guidelines: Dilemmas of formal rationality and sentencing disparity. *Criminology, 34*(3), 306–332.

Ulmer, J. T., & Kramer, J. H. (1998). The use and transformation of formal decision making criteria: Sentencing guidelines, organizational contexts, and case processing strategies. *Social Problems, 45*(2), 248–267.

Appendix 5

Langan, P. A., & Levin, D. J. (2002). *Recidivism of prisoners released in 1994.* (NCJ 193427). Washington, DC: Bureau of Justice Statistics.

Sabol, W. J., Couture, H., & Harrison, P. M. (2007). *Prisoners in 2006.* (NCJ 219416). Washington DC: Bureau of Justice Statistics.

Index

CPSIA information can be obtained at www.ICGtesting.com
Printed in the USA
BVOW032118260312

286011BV00006B/1/P

9 780199 782857